T0284556

Heiner Müller
After Shakespeare

Heiner Müller
After Shakespeare

MACBETH
◊
ANATOMY TITUS FALL OF ROME

TRANSLATED BY
Carl Weber
Paul David Young

New York, New York

Heiner Müller After Shakespeare © 2012 PAJ Publications
© 2012 Carl Weber, Introduction and translation of *Macbeth* and *Shakespeare a Difference*
© 2012 Carl Weber and Paul David Young, translation of *Anatomy Titus Fall of Rome*

Macbeth © Suhrkamp Verlag Frankfurt am Main 2001
Anatomy of Titus – Fall of Rome © Suhrkamp Verlag Frankfurt am Main 2002
Shakespeare eine Differenz © Suhrkamp Verlag Frankfurt am Main 2005
First Edition

Heiner Müller After Shakespeare is published by PAJ Publications, P.O. Box 532, Village Station, New York, NY 10014. PAJ Publications is distributed to the trade by Consortium Book Sales and Distribution: www.cbsd.com

Publisher of PAJ Publications: Bonnie Marranca

The translations in this volume have been supported by funds from the Goethe-Institut. This publication is made possible with public funds from the New York State Council on the Arts, a state agency.

Library of Congress Cataloging-in-Publication Data

Müller, Heiner, 1929-1995.
[Plays. English. Selections]
Heiner Müller after Shakespeare : Macbeth and Anatomy Titus - Fall of Rome / Heiner Müller ; translated by Carl Weber and Paul David Young.
    p. cm.
 ISBN 978-1-55554-152-1
 I. Weber, Carl. II. Young, Paul David. III. Title.
 PT2673.U29A2 2012
  832'.914--dc23
                        2012021533

Contents

A Life-long Discourse with Shakespeare
◊
Carl Weber

Heiner Müller was thirteen-years-old when he read *Hamlet* in its English original for the first time, despite the warning of one of his teachers that the text would be too difficult for him. As he later noted: "I guessed more than I actually understood, but the leap creates an experience, not the step."

Throughout his life as a writer, he was to continue what could be called a "discourse" with Shakespeare's work, by way of public statements and, foremost, in his writings. He adapted what he considered Shakespeare's worldview, as he perceived it, in the texts of the Bard from his own perspective of living in the Europe of the twentieth century. It was a life that he defined with the title of his autobiography: *War without Battle. Life in Two Dictatorships.* His perspective corresponded closely to the one articulated by the Polish critic Jan Kott in his seminal book *Shakespeare Our Contemporary.*

Shakespeare a Difference, the text of an address Müller gave at a conference of Shakespeare scholars, *Shakespeare Tage*, in Weimar, April 1988, appears in this volume with his plays. It was delivered less than two years before the fall of the Berlin Wall, and alludes to "Real Existing Socialism," the ruling party SED's characterization of the socio-economic system in the DDR. Among the historical figures mentioned in the text are Pol Pot, Friedrich Hölderlin, Friedrich Nietzsche, W. H. Auden, and Vasily Grossman. Müller often quotes the original English, whose passages are indicated by asterisks. He writes: "Shakespeare is a mirror through the ages, our hope a world he doesn't reflect anymore. We haven't arrived at ourselves as long as Shakespeare is writing our plays."

Already in his early years as a writer, in 1950, Müller attempted an adaptation of *Timon of Athens.* He completed only the opening scene of a text he titled *The Golden Calf.* Judging from the few extant pages, he aspired to write a satiric comment on capitalism's treatment of the arts and artists as commodities. But he then turned to writing plays—and poetry—that reflected and critically observed the creation of a Socialist economy and its corresponding

1

society in the young East-German state GDR, which had to be achieved with a citizenry who in their majority had been Nazis or more or less loyal to Hitler's Nazi system. Müller was fully committed to the new socialist society and refused to join his parents when they defected to capitalist West Germany.

Deeply impressed by Brecht's theatre at the Berliner Ensemble, Müller emulated a Brechtian dramaturgy in the plays he wrote during the fifties, texts that dealt with the societal changes and the ensuing problems of the East-German Socialist republic. However, he increasingly adopted what could be called Shakespeare's dramatic model, beginning with *The Resettled Woman or Life in the Countryside*. He himself called this satiric comedy in fifteen scenes about the quandaries of early post-war East-German agriculture, from the 1946 Socialist land reform to the government-enforced transition to collective farming in 1960, "a history, a play in a Shakespeare dramaturgy." In the character of the alcoholic Fondrak, who leaves the GDR for the West, Müller created a contemporary character quite comparable to Shakespeare's fools. The first production of the play, in the fall of 1961, was closed by the cultural government authorities after one preview and resulted in Müller's exclusion from the Writers Association, in addition to an extended period during which his texts could neither be published nor performed in the GDR. In his next play about societal controversies during East Germany's early decade, *The Construction Site* of 1965. It could not be performed in the GDR until 1980. Müller employed nearly throughout Shakespearean blank verse to structure a realistic contemporary dialogue.

In the sixties during which his own writings were banned in the GDR, Müller tried to support himself by doing translations, from the works of Sophocles, Molière, Chekhov and Mayakovsky. His commissioned literal translation of *As You Like It* successfully premiered at the Residenz Theater of Munich in 1968. It was Müller's first truly close encounter with a Shakespeare text. He observed: "It was [an experience] as if I worked in his body. I obtained a feeling for the double sexuality, the combination of snakes and beasts of prey in his language, in the dramaturgy of his plays. Since then I believed I knew him personally." Müller discovered in Shakespeare, as he later claimed, an "antidote" to Brecht who had been his revered model since he began to write for the theatre.

In 1969, he had occasion to closely examine the narrative of *A Midsummer Night's Dream*, within a contemporary GDR context, in a play called *Horizons*. The text, written by Gerhard Winterlich, transposed the summer-night scenes from Shakespeare's forest to an East German environment, for a performance Winterlich had staged with amateur actors, namely the workers of a petroleum refinery. In this performance the summer night events took place in the East German countryside near the refinery, during a holiday weekend. The artistic director of the East Berlin Volksbühne Theater, Benno Besson, asked Müller to rework Winterlich's text for a professional production he was to direct at his theatre, in 1969. The performance as much as Müller's version of the play were rejected by critics and audiences.

In 1970, Müller got word that the theatre in the provincial town of Brandenburg planned a production of *Macbeth* for the 1971-72 season. He offered, and was invited, to provide a new translation of the Shakespeare play. Starting with the text of the first scene, he recognized that he could not leave it as is: "I would have to fully accept this idea of predestination, that the chain of events is programmed by supernatural forces. Therefore I first eliminated that scene, and this resulted in an increasing number of changes." Among the features that he felt needed change he cited Shakespeare's belief in the divine institution of kings and the total absence of Scotland's underclass in the narrative. While working on his adaptation, Müller went back to Shakespeare's source for the text, Holinshed's *Chronicles of England, Scotland and Ireland.*

The Brandenburg premiere of his play, in 1972, triggered an animated controversial debate among critics and scholars with extremely opposing responses. Some reviews welcomed Müller's *Macbeth after Shakespeare* as a play in its own right, while others rejected the adaptation and accused Müller of "historical pessimism" and the lack of a humanistic worldview. Müller rejected such criticism: "In *Macbeth* there is an optimistic element of history, the witches. Every revolution needs a destructive element, and in my play that is the witches, they destroy without exception all those who possess power."

Müller added a significant number of new scenes to the text and introduced with them numerous characters from the lower classes. Whereas in Shakespeare we witness exclusively the conflicts among Scotland's ruling class, Müller's lower-class characters, be they peasants, servants or soldiers, are in no way idealized. They are brutalized by the ruling aristocracy, and they themselves in turn brutalize their own kind. This quite realistic perspective was rejected by some East German critics, who claimed the text was "inadequate as a Socialist interpretation of Shakespeare." The play received a number of West German productions, and there the critical reception was often equally negative and the text was dismissed as "too brutal."

In 1982, Heiner Müller himself staged the play at the East Berlin Volksbühne (where the artistic director, Benno Besson, had hired him as the company's dramaturg), in collaboration with his then wife Ginka Cholakova. He remembered in his autobiography the performance as "a medium-sized scandal." The set represented the inner court of a typical Berlin working class apartment building, with a telephone booth, the metal poles to hang carpets for beating them clean, and trash heaps. The role of Macbeth was cast with three actors to highlight the diverse components of the character's narrative. Müller wanted to shift the focus from a single individual character and instead emphasize the recurrent structure and mechanisms of the power struggles in the play. He later remarked: "One can say a lot of things about Stalin with a production of *Macbeth.*" He also complained that the comic aspects of the performance had not been perceived, namely that in his production "the power struggles of the ruling class were viewed with a sneering perspective from below." Müller viewed his production in the tradition of a "popular theatre" where, as he wrote, the performance *Gestus* is derived "from the Grand Guignol rather than [the poetic style of] the Bread and Puppet Theatre."

In May, 2011, the English version published in this volume had its world premiere in Vancouver, BC, Canada, in a joint production by Theatre Conspiracy and GasHeart Theatre, who commissioned the translation. A reviewer for the *Vancouver Courier* described the production, whose staging "incorporated some high tech features ... along with contemporary costumes and hand-guns, bringing the play forward in time ... Duncan is flanked by closed circuit monitors that show the war raging outside. Macbeth converses to Lady Macbeth via webcam ... *Macbeth nach Shakespeare* is potent stuff ... warning that abuse of power extends into the computer age.*"

Several years before Müller directed his *Macbeth* production at the Volksbühne, Benno Besson had planned a staging of *Hamlet* for the 1976/77 season at his theatre. He asked Müller to provide a new translation. Müller collaborated with the young director/dramaturg Matthias Langhoff while translating *The Tragic History of Hamlet Prince of Denmark*. The translation kept particularly close to the English of Shakespeare's original, often crafting what might be called an Anglicized German, for instance, by retaining the present participle so frequent in Shakespeare but rarely used in German speech and literature. Their view of the play was strongly influenced by Jan Kott's then just published study *Shakespeare Our Contemporary* (1964), in which Kott compared the informants employed by Claudius, Rosencrantz and Guildenstern as well as Horatio, to the contemporary secret police system prevalent at the time in the East European socialist states.

While working on the translation of Shakespeare's play, Müller started to think about inserting a Hamlet character into recent historical events in Communist Eastern Europe. Langhoff, who worked daily with Müller on the translation, reports that, while doing the translation, Müller began to write an "East European" Hamlet play. During his first visit to the U.S., where he had been invited as a resident writer at the University of Texas-Austin, he concluded work on the performance text that he later was to call *Hamletmachine*. It was finished in 1977, after Müller's sojourn in the U.S. In the new text, with the exception of a few quotes, little of the original was left of Shakespeare. However, seven verses of a poem dedicated to Shakespeare's *Hamlet*, that Müller had written in the late fifties, reappeared in *Hamletmachine* as the concluding lines.[1]

---

[1] Heiner Müller, *Hamletmachine and Other Texts for the Stage*. New York: PAJ Publications, 1984.

Müller found striking the similarity of the burial of Hamlet's father and the 1956 state funeral for the former Hungarian foreign minister, Lazlo Rajk, in Budapest. Rajk had been rehabilitated after having been executed subsequent to a Stalinist show trial in 1949. During the funeral procession, Rajk's widow and son walked behind the coffin. This event became a trigger for the Hungarian revolution of October 1956. Originally, Müller's intended title was *Hamlet in Budapest*. Müller incorporated into the text many allusions to the East German uprising of June 1953 when he, a convinced believer in the GDR's Socialist system, nevertheless felt a great deal of empathy for the striking workers and their grievances.

After beginning with many evocations of the character Hamlet, the text focuses on the character of Ophelia and eventually cites women from the twentieth century who had been murdered or committed suicide, among them Rosa Luxemburg (the German-Polish Communist leader assassinated in 1919) and Müller's second wife, Inge Müller (who killed herself using a gas stove in 1966, during the years his writings were banned in the GDR.) The piece ends with Ophelia, tied to a wheelchair and wrapped in gauze who, calling herself "Electra," conjures a women's revolt against the male-dominated world. While spending time in the U.S., Müller had observed the highly active feminism of the seventies. He told me at the time that in an American production Ophelia rather than Hamlet ought to be the protagonist.

The text's first American production of note was staged, in 1986, by Robert Wilson with students of the Tisch School of the Arts at New York University. The performance attracted considerable critical attention and established Müller in the U.S. as an important author of late-twentieth century theatre. It resulted in his being the most frequently performed German playwright in North America for many years. Soon Wilson and Müller became close friends, working together on several other productions, including *Alcestis*, *The CIVIL WarS*, *The Forest*. Since Müller's death in 1995, Wilson has also staged his earlier play *Quartet*, in Paris, with Isabelle Huppert, having previously directed its American premiere two decades earlier with Lucinda Childs.

One reason Müller remained attracted to *Hamlet* throughout his life (and worked on several German versions of the Shakespeare text) was that he regarded Hamlet as the prototype of the German intellectual who, in several historical incarnations—from Lessing to Heidegger and Brecht and up to Müller himself—tried to influence or even define the politics of their governing powers, but always failed in the endeavor. In Müller's view, their failure facilitated many of the aberrations that characterized German history.

Müller himself first directed the text of *Hamletmachine* with the theatre institute students at the University of Giessen, Germany, in 1985. Five years later, in 1989-90, he staged a combination of *Hamlet* and *Hamletmachine* at Berlin's Deutsches Theater. During the rehearsal period the socialist East German republic imploded, due to massive demonstrations of its citizens, the exodus of many thousands of them, and the collapse of the Berlin Wall. The daily shifting events necessitated continuing changes of text and performance details in rehearsal. Eventually the show became an eight-hour performance, with Ulrich Mühe, who was later to gain international recognition for his performance in the Academy Award-winning German film, *The Lives of Others*, playing an unforgettable Hamlet. Müller put the text of *Hamletmachine* into Shakespeare's play before the final act. The production explored Kott's reading of the text, which saw Horatio, Rosencrantz and Guildenstern as agents of Claudius' secret security police, demonstrating Müller's view of Hamlet as he expressed it in *Hamletmachine*. It is unfortunate that we won't know how Müller's view of Hamlet might have changed in the vastly different historical landscape of the new century, against the background of evolving events in the Muslim world.

However, in the next, and his last, adaptation of a Shakespeare play we find evidence that he recognized the growing power of non-Western peoples and the implications of their increasingly anti-Western attitude. In 1984, Müller was asked to provide a Shakespeare adaptation for the city of Bochum's company in West Germany, and offered to revive an old project, namely the re-reading of one of Shakespeare's earliest plays, *Titus Andronicus*, that would establish a context making audiences understand it as a comment on contemporary history. The adaptation, *Anatomy Titus Fall of Rome A Shakespeare*

Commentary, reflected on the emerging Third World during the second part of the twentieth century, personified in the character of the Moor, Aaron. The text also anticipated an end of Western/American dominance of non-Western societies—be they in Asia, Latin America, or Africa—and the impact of mass immigration: The barbarian Goths under command of the Roman general Titus' son, who had defected from Rome, conquer and occupy the former capital as the new rulers of the Roman world.

The play's narrative is the most bloody and violent of the Shakespeare canon and Müller's version even increases the goriness of the play's events that are triggered by the competition of revenge taking place between Titus and the Gothic queen Tamora, culminating in Titus serving Tamora the flesh of her own sons for dinner. Shakespeare's play has been compared to our contemporary genre of horror movies, and Müller's text shows the influence of this interpretation.

The treatment of Shakespeare's *Titus Andronicus* is in its formal structure positioned between Müller's *Macbeth* version and the complete remake of *Hamlet* in *Hamletmachine*. Müller brought into the original text narrative segments, often indicated by the exclusive use of capitals, but also returns at times to a quite literal rendering of Shakespeare's text. As later with the Berlin *Hamlet* production, the play was continually reworked during rehearsals. Using one of Kafka's well-known aphorisms, Müller noted about the play that "T.A. is not a bird / in search of a cage but a cage / in search of a bird. (A form/structure is searching its content.)" The play premiered at the Bochum Kammerspiele in 1985, directed by B. K. Tragelehn, who had staged the embattled performance of *The Resettled Woman*, twenty-five years earlier. It received its GDR premiere at the Staatsschauspiel Dresden, in 1987, directed by Wolfgang Engel, who interpreted the play as a reading and partial enacting of the text by students in a high-school class, an approach that emphasized Müller's combination of straight narrative segments with fully performed scenes.

Anatomy Titus ... was to be Müller's last adaptation of a Shakespeare play. Judging from several of his notes, he was considering work on Shakespeare's last completed play, *The Tempest,* as indicated by the last poem he wrote:

> Go Ariel bring the storm
>   to silence and
> throw the numbed ones on the beach
>   I need them
>   alive, that I can kill them
>
>
>   Me   Father
>   why

At the time, 1995, he had become the artistic director of the Berliner Ensemble, and finally assumed what could be considered as "Brecht's mantle." The new responsibilities and the requisite directorial obligations—he staged several plays by himself and also by Brecht in the last year of his life—hardly offered him the time to work on a new Shakespeare project. However, he did announce as the prospective repertoire of the Ensemble: Brecht, Shakespeare and Müller, an indication that further appropriations of Shakespeare texts were on his mind. We have to regret that his death that same year prevented a continued discourse with Shakespeare's theatre. The two plays in this volume demonstrate the extraordinary achievement that Müller's life-long discourse with Shakespeare has yielded.

On translation:
In the texts, stage directions are indicated by italics, as Müller did. He did not specify a character's entrance by the word "enter." In general, characters use the word "you" to address each other, though Müller's texts naturally employ the several German variations on the word "you" to indicate status, familiarity or plurality (du, ihr, Sie).

9

MACBETH
After Shakespeare

◊

Translated by Carl Weber

CHARACTERS

MACBETH

DUNCAN

MALCOLM

DONALBAIN

BANQUO

FLEANCE

MACDUFF

LENOX

ROSSE

ANGUS

A LORD

SEYTON

PHYSICIAN

PORTER

LADY MACBETH

LADY MACDUFF

LADY-IN-WAITING

THREE WITCHES

LORDS, LADIES, MURDERERS, SERVANTS, SOLDIERS,
    PEASANTS, ET AL.

1

Duncan. Malcolm. Lenox. Soldiers.

DUNCAN   What bloody man comes here? Such costume pledges
The newest state of the revolt
MALCOLM   This soldier fought
'Gainst my captivity. Friend, tell thy king
How does the battle go.
SOLDIER   On the seesaw.
That dog Macdonwald who has cooked this stew
Gathers Scotland's dregs like offal attracts flies,
And fortune was his whore until Macbeth
Made him taste his sword steaming from gored flesh.
See, our man disdaining fortune waded
Through corpses with his bloody tool until
He had the mutineer before his steel and
Sliced him up from nave to chops as if
It were a handshake, like this
Demonstrates it and keels over while doing so:
And then upon our banner fixed his head.
DUNCAN   Oh good Macbeth.
SOLDIER   That's the beginning. Barely
Had the just cause with blood and steel made run
The Scottish serf, the king of Norway, keen
On his advantage, with arms drawn and new
Supplies of men began a fresh assault.
DUNCAN   Vexed this our commanders courage, Macbeth
And Banquo?
SOLDIER   As sparrows eagles would. If you
Ask me: Like two overcharged cannons they

13

Attacked removing foe and foe, four handed
As if they meant to bathe in putrid wounds
And throw dice with bones at Golgatha
Or whatever. You hear my gashes cry
For help.
DUNCAN They talk as loudly as thy word
Of honor. Go get him surgeons. Who comes here.
MALCOLM The Thane of Rosse.
LENOX He has a hasty look and
Seems to be full of news.
Rosse.
ROSSE God save the King.
DUNCAN Where from, Thane.
ROSSE From your battle, great King
Where Norway's banners are like our sky
And fan our people cold. Norway himself
With terrifying numbers, and assisted
By Cawdor, that most disloyal traitor,
Started the bloody dance. But our Macbeth
Sword against sword, arm against arm, pushed down
His neck unto our Scottish earth.
In brief: victory fell on us.
DUNCAN I call that
Great happiness.
ROSSE So that Norway's king
Is whining now for peace. And we refuse
Him for his dead a single hole in the
Blood soaked field until he has disbursed
Ten thousand thalers into our hands.
DUNCAN No more that Thane of Cawdor shall worry
Our heart. Go and pronounce his present death
And with his former title greet Macbeth.

ROSSE   I go and see it will at once be done.

DUNCAN   What that dog lost, the hero now has won.

2

Witches

WITCH 1   You hear the drumming between day and night.

WITCH 2   Lost as well as won has been the battle.

WITCH 3   Sister, where is the blood from on thy garment.

WITCH 1   I had my banquet on the battlefield.

WITCH 2   Sister, what is the thing that's in your hand.

WITCH 3   A pilot's thumb. I threw his ship on the beach.

WITCH 1   What kind of doll, Sister, is in your arm.

WITCH 2   My king, sweetheart.

WITCH 3   Come, old man, we'll make you warm.

They burn a doll: King Duncan.

Macbeth and Banquo.

MACBETH   I have not seen a day so fair and foul.

BANQUO   How long the way to Forres. Who are these.

So gray and shrunken in their wild attire.

And not like anything that lives on earth

And yet are on it. Live you. Are you a thing that

A man may question. Hey, they understand me

They lay their rough finger on skinny lips

Each one. Women. Their beards say something else

What image in the fire. It's like the king.

What are you doing with his Majesty's image.

MACBETH   Who are you. If you've got language, speak.

WITCH 1   All hail Macbeth, Thane of Glamis.

WITCH 2   And of Cawdor.

WITCH 3   All hail Macbeth, king of Scotland.

BANQUO Why

Comrade, do you fear things that sound so fair.

In the name of truth: are you what you seem to be

Or just madness. My noble partner here

You greet with present grace and great prediction

Of higher rank as well as royal hope

That he won't know himself. You tell me nothing.

If you can peek into the seeds of time

Know which grain will grow up and which will not

Speak to me, who neither seeks nor fears

Favors or hate from you.

WITCH 1 Hail Banquo, lesser than Macbeth and more.

WITCH 2 Less happy, yet happier than him.

WITCH 3 Kings you'll beget though you yourself are none.

ALL WITCHES Hail Macbeth and Banquo. Banquo and Macbeth.

MACBETH Reticent speakers. Stay and tell me more.

After my father I am Thane of Glamis

But how of Cawdor. The Thane of Cawdor lives,

In blooming health. And that I shall be king

Is less believable than Cawdor. Tell me

Wherefrom you've got this strange knowledge, and why

Upon this blasted heath you block our way

With a prophetic greeting. Speak, I implore you.

Witches vanish.

BANQUO The earth drives bubbles as the water does and

They were of such kind. They are gone. Where to.

MACBETH Like breath, into the wind. I wish they'd stayed.

BANQUO Was real what we talk about now. Or

Have we eaten of the sick'ning root

That makes a prisoner of our reason.

MACBETH Your children shall be kings.

BANQUO And you king.

16

MACBETH   And Thane of Cawdor. Was it not so.
BANQUO   Like that
Were their tune and words. But who comes here.
ROSSE and ANGUS.
ROSSE   Macbeth. Your king has happily received
News of his victory, and balancing
Your part, he wonders what is yours, what's his.
Sure of this, he sees
You that same day in Norway's battle ranks
Without any fear of your own labor:
Images of death. As thick as hail appear
To him messengers, every one full of
Your glory in his Majesty's defense
And spit it out before him.
ANGUS   We are sent
To forward thanks to you from our king
And then to escort you into his sight,
Not to reward you.
ROSSE   And as a handout of a greater honor
Accept these greetings as the Thane of Cawdor.
Good luck with the promotion.
BANQUO   Does the devil
Speak true.
MACBETH   The Thane of Cawdor lives. You clothe me
With borrowed glamour.
ANGUS   He who was Thane of Cawdor
Lives under the axe. If he was aligned with
Norway, or if he stiffened the plebeians'
Back with hidden help, or if he has
Labored with both at his country's ruin,
I know not and I don't know who knows it.
But it has been confessed and is confirmed

His high treason.

MACBETH   Glamis. And Thane of Cawdor.

The greatest will still come. Thanks for your pains.

To Banquo:

Do you not hope now that your brood will moult

Themselves, in order to be royalty.

Those, who made me Thane of Cawdor, promised

No less than that.

BANQUO   Are you not keen, Thane, for

Our king Duncan's crown.

To Rosse and Angus:

A word, good Sirs.

MACBETH   Two times the truth. A happy prologue to

The game of power. Many thanks, my friends.

This supernatural soliciting

Cannot be ill; cannot be good. If ill,

Why the advance: I am the Thane of Cawdor.

If good, why does my skin shiver against it

And my sitting heart beat at my ribs

Loudly against nature. Terrors lived through

Are fairy tales of gruesome fantasy.

My plan, where murder has not yet a body

Shakes my lonely human mind so much that

Anticipation stops and nothing is

But what it is not.

BANQUO   The man, you see, is rapt.

MACBETH   If you want me king, chance, give me the crown

Spare me the grab.

BANQUO   New honors come upon us

Like our garments, strange, until their use

Made them fit the bearer.

MACBETH   Come what may come

18

Time runs with hours through the roughest day.
BANQUO The King is waiting for the Thane of Cawdor.

3

Duncan, seated on corpses that have been stacked to create a throne. Malcolm.

DUNCAN Is Cawdor yet under the axe. Where are those
We have commissioned with his death. His head.
Lenox.
LENOX Here, my king. And I who saw him die
Can report that frankly he confessed his
Treason and implored your Highness' pardon
Crawling on his knees. In his life nothing
Became him like his leaving it. He died
As one who had been trained to die, throwing
Away the dearest property he owned
Like a piece of rags.
DUNCAN No art can read
Within the face what moves a person's mind.
Boxes the ears of the head.
He was a man on whom I built my sleep.
Macbeth, Banquo. Duncan lets the head drop.
Macbeth, my most worthy commander.
I've born heavy my sin of thanklessness
Right now. So far ahead of me you are
That with the swiftest wing your recompense
Won't overtake you. Had you but less deserved,
The balance would be in my hand. I know
That more than all I own won't pay your prize.
MACBETH The service and the loyalty I owe
Will pay itself and Your Highness part is

That you insist upon our duties; which are

Children and servants to your throne and state.

DUNCAN   I have planted you and my labor shall

Be your further growth. Most noble Banquo,

You have deserved no less and take your seat now

Within my heart.

BANQUO   A high place to inhabit.

High or low, whatever I will bring in

The harvest will be yours.

Duncan embraces by turns Macbeth and Banquo. Soldiers with captured

Peasants, bound by ropes.

SOLDIER   That's what left of them.

MALCOLM   Hang them.

SOLDIER   Are we to drag them across half of Scotland.

The land's been razed. One victory after another.

Here grass won't grow now.

MALCOLM   Throw them into the swamp.

It is nearby. Beat drums if they should scream

While the king holds court.

Soldiers drag the Peasants away. Screams of the drowning during the following

dialogue. Drums.

DUNCAN   Friends, my luck

Overflows, dressing itself in tears.

Sons, thanes, all you close to our throne,

Know: We will bequeath our state upon

Our firstborn. Malcolm, to be named hereafter

The Prince of Cumberland, which honor shall

Not be shared and due alone to him.

The signs of nobility, like stars, shall shine

On every merit. From here to Inverness

That we owe and more to the Thane of Cawdor.

MACBETH   I shall be your messenger and bring

My wife the joyful news of your arrival.
Exit.
DUNCAN True, good Banquo, he's all nobility.
To sing his praise will be a feast to me.
Let's follow him, who fits the bed for us.

4

Soldiers throw Peasants into the swamp. Macbeth.

MACBETH The Prince of Cumberland. That step blocks me.
The one who has to fall or leap, am I.
Star and star, go and put out your fires
That light won't see my black and deep desires.
Eye, forget the hand. Let happen that
Which, when done, the eye refuses to see.
Exit.

5

Lady Macbeth, reading a letter.

LADY MACBETH "They met me on the day of victory, and I know from
the most precise example, they have more than mortal knowledge. When
I burned with desire to question them further, they made themselves into
air, wherein they vanished. While I stood still spellbound, messengers from
the king arrived, who hailed me Thane of Cawdor, which title my sisters,
the witches, had before bestowed on me, pointing at the time to come with
Hail king, who shall be. I thought it good to tell you this, partner of my
greatness. Put it close to your heart and farewell."
Glamis you are, and Cawdor. And shall be
What you are destined for. Would not your mind be

All too full with milk of love for humans
To walk the straight on way. Grab the crown
You want with spotless hand, and don't play false.
Yet as to winning, you need, great Glamis
What screams at you: That, if you want it, do it
And what you're more afraid of doing than
That you want it not done. What are the tidings .
Servant.
SERVANT   The King comes here tonight.
LADY MACBETH   Madness rides you.
Is not your master with him, who, were it true
Would have informed us, so we can prepare us.
SERVANT   Forgive me, it is true. The Thane is coming.
One of ours rode ahead of him
Who barely had breath left after his ride
To pass on the message.
Exit.
LADY MACBETH   Even the raven
Is hoarse, that croaks Duncan's fatal entrance
Under my battlements.
Macbeth.
Great Glamis. Cawdor.
Greater than both you're with tomorrow's greetings.
Your letter has transported me beyond
This dull today, and the present moment
Has taste of the future.
MACBETH   Duncan comes
Here tonight.
LADY MACBETH   When does he leave.
MACBETH   Tomorrow, as he wants.
LADY MACBETH   Never the sun shall look at this tomorrow.
Close up your face, Thane, it is like a book

Where everyone can read peculiar matters.
Deceiving time, deceive you like the time.
Look like a flower, be below the serpent.
He who comes must be provided for.
This night's great business leave to my hand, Thane.
MACBETH   We will speak further of it.
Screaming outside.
LADY MACBETH   What noise is that.
MACBETH   A peasant who paid not his tenant rent.
LADY MACBETH   I want to see him bleed, to train my eye
For the painting we have to do tonight.
MACBETH   I'll have him brought here, since you want it so.
Exit.
LADY MACBETH   Macbeth. King of Scotland.
Two Servants with the flogged Peasant. Macbeth.
MACBETH   Your peasant, Lady.
Lady Macbeth covers her eyes with her hands. Macbeth laughs.

6

Peasant in the stocks. Duncanand Banquo.

DUNCAN   This castle has a pleasant seat. The air here
Recommends itself to our senses.
BANQUO   The summer guest that loves to nest at churches
The swallow, shows with lots of masonry
That heaven here is breathing well. No buttress
Where the bird has not built his hanging bed
And breeding cradle. I have always noticed
That where they are breeding most diligently
The air is best.
Lady Macbeth.

DUNCAN   Our most handsome hostess.
A burden sometimes is the love we feel
Yet we allow it as love. Learn from me
To bid God he'll reward you for your pains
And thank us for your trouble.
LADY MACBETH   All our service
Twice done in every point, and then done double
Is a poor single deed against the honors
Your Majesty is loading our house with.
For former high regards, and heaped upon them
The latest, we'll remain your debtors.
DUNCAN   Where is
The Thane of Cawdor. We followed him closely
Wanting to announce him. But he rides well
And his love, as sharp as his spurs, gave him
The start on us. Fair and noble hostess
We are your guest tonight.
LADY MACBETH   Your servants ever
Have what is ours and ourselves as fief
And will repay it at your Highness' pleasure
Giving to you what is yours.
DUNCAN   Your hand.
Conduct me to my host. We love him dearly
And our grace continues to shine on him.
By your leave, Lady.

7

Servants pass by, carrying butchered animals. Macbeth.

MACBETH   I was his butcher. Why not his carrion
On my hook. I've fortified his throne

And have raised it with the heaps of corpses.
If I took back all my bloody work
His place would long have been below the earth.
He pays me what he owes me, when I do it.
If it were done when it is done, it's good
And done fast. If murder could enshrine
What murder breeds, that but this single blow
Might be the be-all and end-all,
And only on this rusty workbench time
We'd leap with ease unto the life to come.
As well, nobody has come back from there
To tell us that it's there. Maybe there is none.
But for such cases there is judgment here
The bloody lessons come to beat the teacher
Reprisal even-handed stuffs the poison
Down into our teeth. He is here
Doubly protected: I am his subject
That blunts the dagger's tip, and I'm his host
Who should against his murderer shut the gate
Instead of grab and wield the knife myself.
Besides, this Duncan looks like snow so clean
That all the blood upon his claws is now
Believed no more. Even that snow is screaming
Against the black evil of his slaughter.
And pity like a naked newborn babe
The storm its belly, or on unseen horses,
Made of air, the angels themselves blow
Into every eye the horrid deed, that
Tears shall drown the wind. I have no spur
To prick the sides of my will, only this
Hasty ambition.
Lady Macbeth.

How now. Do you want the news?
LADY MACBETH   He has eaten. Tomorrow we will eat
From his silver. Why did you go away.
MACBETH   Did he ask for me.
LADY MACBETH   Don't you know he did.
MACBETH   We will proceed no further in this matter.
He has paid me well, and golden praise
Have I acquired from all kind of people
And as you know with small coinage this time
I have had other creases in my flesh.
The fresh luster wants to be worn down
Not thrown away still new.
LADY MACBETH   Was the hope beer fumes
Which puffed you up, somewhat like a sleep,
That in daylight it gapes green and pale
At what it did freely. And that much I know
Of your love now. Are you afraid, Macbeth,
To be the man you are when you are dreaming.
He itches and he is afraid to scratch.
Some blood might get under his fingernail.
So live then with your craving for the crown
Gauge your horniness against your cowardice
Still waiting with I-dare-not for I-want-to.
MACBETH   Be silent. I dare all that is right for
A man. Who dares do more is none.
LADY MACBETH   What creature
Has then revealed this enterprise to me.
You were a man while daring it, the more so
You will be the man who is more than you.
No time nor place have been propitious then
You wanted to force both into your fist.
They offer themselves and you have no fist now.

26

You've butchered for him, and the stench of blood
Still was in our embrace. Dare it for yourself.
I have given suck and know how sweet love
Tastes for the babe that milks me. I would have
Seen his smile yet still would pluck my nipple
From his boneless gums and dash his brains out,
Had I sworn the way you did.
MACBETH   If we fail.
LADY MACBETH   We fail. Just take your courage into pincers
And nothing will fail. When Duncan sleeps, and
After a day on horseback sleep comes quickly,
I shall with spice and wine so persuade
His two chamberlains that their poor mind
Or what is taken for it, is a fog
Their skull a tub of murk. When swinish sleep
Has drowned them that they lie there like in death,
What cannot you and I do then to the
Quite unprotected Duncan, what not blame
On his drunken servants, who shall bear
The guilt of our great scrub.
MACBETH   You shall give
Birth to sons for me. Males only shall grow,
Woman, from your wild guts. Who won't believe
When in his chamber we painted the sleepy
Two with his blood we have drawn with their daggers
That they have done the thrust.
LADY MACBETH   Who'd think it different.
When we with luck have done it and are howling
Our grief about it.

8

Banquo. Fleance.

BANQUO How old is the night, son.
FLEANCE The moon is down.
BANQUO It's down at midnight.
FLEANCE I think it's later, Sir.
BANQUO You take my sword. There is thrift in heaven.
Out all the candles. Take that too. A heavy
Sleep lies like lead on me. Yet I won't sleep.
Powers of mercy, help me from the black
Thoughts that are rising up in our sleep
From basements of the mind. Give me my sword.
Macbeth. Servant with a torch.
BANQUO Who's there.
MACBETH A friend
BANQUO Sir, you are still awake. The King's to bed.
In better mood than usual: he gave
Rich presents to your servants and he greets
With this here diamond your wife as his
Kindest hostess, he is quite content.
MACBETH So hurried came this visit, that our will
Became the only servant of our want.
Else we had shown us more abundant.
BANQUO It was
Enough abundant. I dreamt last night, Macbeth
Of the three Weird Sisters. To you they have
Promised a lot.
MACBETH I do not think of them.
Yet when our service offers us an hour

We should spend some words on this business
If you allow the time.
BANQUO   At your leisure.
MACBETH
Brace my back when the time comes. It will
Provide much honor for you.
BANQUO   If I won't lose
Honor while grasping for more honor and
Still keep allegiance, you can count on me.
MACBETH   Till then: Good night.
BANQUO   Thanks, Sir. And also to you.
Exit Banquo and Fleance.
MACBETH   Go bid your mistress, when my drink is ready
She may strike the bell. You go to bed.
Exit Servant.
Is this a dagger. The handle seeks my hand.
Come, you old iron, that exchanges kings
Midwife of Majesty, heir to the throne.
I do not have you, yet I see you well.
Aren't you real to the hand as to
The eye, fatal image. Are you a dagger
Of dreams, a fake creation born from my
Overheated skull. I still see you
And you are formed as palpable as any
Dagger firmly resting in my hand.
You walk for me the way that I was going.
You are the instrument I wanted to use.
My eye is the clown of my other senses
Or worth the rest. I always see you, dagger
On your blade blood that was not there before.
From your handle there is sweat on my hand
Of murderers before me. How long have you

Like a harlot passed from hand to hand and
Tapped the blood of kings, red as other blood.
I've seen you long enough. You don't exist.
My bloody business teaches thus my eyes.
In the half-world where my body hangs
In nothingness what lives pretends to be dead,
Dreams are riding my sleep, my sisters
The witches, enter now their service, murder
Is cheap, glued with blood the dusty globe now
Swallows its steps. Walk thy walk, signpost
To power, maybe tomorrow into my back.
Enough of words for one single death.
The world has no exit but to the knacker.
With knives into the knife, that is the way.
A bell.
That is the bell, Duncan, it does invite us
To heaven or to hell. Say now your prayers.
Exit. Lady Macbeth.
LADY MACBETH   He is at his work.
The doors are open, and his drunken servants
Do mock their charge with snores. I've drugged their nightcap
So death and sleep are now at loggerheads
For their corpses.
A VOICE   Who is there. What, ho.
LADY MACBETH   Alack. They are awake and it is not
Done. The attempt, and not the deed, confounds us.
I laid their daggers ready for his hand.
He could not miss them. Had he not resembled
My father as he slept, I would have done it.
Is it you, husband.
MACBETH   I've done the deed. If only
I could pour back again his blood into

30

His veins.

LADY MACBETH   What for.

MACBETH *looks at his hands:* This is a sorry sight.

LADY MACBETH   This is the crown.

MACBETH   I have butchered with these selfsame hands
What came before my sword. Thus bathed in blood
In his service my hands have been white.
I was his sword. A sword does have no nose
For the stench from opened bodies. Could I
Cut off the hand that guided me.

LADY MACBETH   You see it.
Your shadow is what blackens now your sun.
For the first time you were your own sword.
Take under your boot now this Scotland and
Black is white.

MACBETH   Have you done it. What do you know.
Who sleeps in the second chamber.

LADY MACBETH   Donalbain
With his servants.

MACBETH   There was someone who
Laughed in his sleep and one cried murder and
They woke themselves up with their own dreams
Each one the other. I stood and heard them.
But they with prayers babbled themselves back
Into their sleep.

LADY MACBETH   That was well prayed.

MACBETH   When I raised up the daggers over him
One cried God-help-us! and Amen! the other.
As if they saw me with these butcher's hands
By what power destined for this purple.
Listening to their fear I could not say
Amen after their God-help-us.

LADY MACBETH   Don't think
About it.
MACBETH   Why could I not say Amen.
LADY MACBETH
I say it for you. Amen. You want it twice.
MACBETH   I had more need of grace but Amen was
Stuck in my throat.
LADY MACBETH   You need Amen no more
After this.
MACBETH   And when I cut his throat
And his blood was gushing over my hands
I heard a voice cry: Sleep no more. Macbeth
Murders the sleep. The sleep that has no guilt
Sleep that calms the turmoil of our grief,
The daily death that is sore laborers' bath,
Balm for heart pain, nature's second course,
And life's main nourishment.
LADY MACBETH   What are you saying.
MACBETH   Always it cried: Sleep no more through this house,
Glamis murders sleep and therefore Cawdor
Shall sleep no more, Macbeth shall sleep no more.
LADY MACBETH   That will be seen, ours is the day.
And save your tears for when they wash the corpse.
A little water shall help the grass grow that
Will sprout from his paunch on top of his gravesite.
Is being your own lord so burdensome.
Don't bend your strength under the usual thinking.
Go get some water and wash from your hand
This grimy evidence. Why do you bring the daggers
Here from their place. Go, carry them back in
And wet his sleepy servants with his blood.
MACBETH   I am afraid to think what I have done

Look at it again, I dare not.

LADY MACBETH   Weak man.

Give me the daggers. Empty pictures are

The sleeping and the dead. The eye of childhood

Fears the painted devil. If the old man still

Has blood, I'll gild the faces of his grooms

That they gleam with guilt.

Exit.

MACBETH   What noise. Who's knocking

Out of my night or is it in your night.

My heart that dog or someone at the south gate.

Who wants on the butcher's bench. Hey you,

Make less noise. The corpse is new at his job,

Forgetting his fresh dignity he could rise,

His head, hair down, dangling from his neck

By the three tendons that my cut has saved.

What happened that each noise will frighten me

And grab me with frog fingers by my neck.

What has not happened yet. What hands have been

Planted here for me and are spooning

Now my eyes out. Hand or eye.

What do I need eyes to see this spot.

Not all the water, when the oceans gather

Will wash my hand quite clean of his blood.

This my hand here will rather dress the sea

In purple, and turn into red the green.

Lady Macbeth.

LADY MACBETH   My hands are of your color. But my shame

Is now my white heart. I hear a knocking

At the south gate. Let's go to our chamber.

A little water cleans us of the deed.

How light a burden it is then. Your will has

Left you quite alone. More knocking. Put on
Your nightgown that chance won't find us awake
Before other sleepers. Do not think
Yourself so deeply into your weakness.
Exit.
MACBETH   To know my deed. The best thing would be now
Not to know myself. Knock from his sleep
The royal corpse. If you but could.

9

Porter.

PORTER   Well knocked, Sir. The knocking has its tune, Sir.
Sings:

> He cut her nipples off with a sword
> A sorry sight to see—

Knock as much as you can, you still have to wait for the porter. That wakes
the dead. You want to get a ghost on your neck.

> And down the lady's heart blood poured
> And dropped from her knees

That must be a peripatetic gentleman who makes such clamor so early. What's
new under the moon that it can't wait for the sun. Hey. I can knock too: my
leg is of Scottish forest like the gate. A forest takes its time, Sir. *Drinks.* That's
a remedy against the forest fire. *Unlocks the gate.*
Macduff and Lenox.
It was my deathwatch beetle, Sirs, that kept you waiting, as for me I am speed
itself in opening gates. Did my leg get into your way, Sir, that you look so
cross. It was a good leg, Sir, until it went astray toward England. There is no
fidelity in a leg, Sir, once it starts running. It lied in, I'm talking of my leg,
Sir, on a battlefield near Bannockbride with an army of English maggots. The
arm, Sir, went rutting in its company, out of love for symmetry.

MACDUFF   Shall I nail you to the gate, porter.
He does so with his sword.
LENOX   I'll have you take to your legs, arm stump. Run.
Hews off his wooden leg. They both laugh.
Macbeth.
LENOX   We had to straighten, Sir, the hands of the clock
For your porter. He limps against the time.
MACBETH   Thanks for your labor.
LENOX   It has been a pleasure.
MACBETH   Labor is labor.
MACDUFF   Labor that is pleasure
Is no labor. Where does the King sleep. He gave
Orders to wake him early.
MACBETH   There is the door.
MACDUFF   I'll dare and wake him, as he ordered me
Exit.
LENOX   The King will ride today?
MACBETH   So he decided.
LENOX   The night has been unruly. At our quarters
The chimney was blown down. The air was full of
Whining, death rattles, never heard the like
Soothsaying in a strange and dreadful sing-song
Of savage fires, reversion of the world's way
Hatched in the womb of time. The night bird screamed
Gaps into our sleep. The servants say
The earth is being drunk from blood and is
Convulsed with cramps.
MACBETH   The night was rough.
LENOX   My young
Remembrance knows of none that's been like this one.
MACBETH   Servants. Clear that away before the King gets
Up so blood will not offend his eye

Though it was spilled for him with hurried zeal.
Servants drag the Porter out, wash the blood off gate and floor.
Macduff.
MACDUFF   You like to drink blood, Thane.
MACBETH   Blood. What do you
Talk of.
LENOX   What has happened.
MACDUFF   Someone is here
Who knows what I talk of. Someone perhaps
Lies in that chamber or this one and grabs
With freshly whitened claws after the crown
And next to him perhaps another one is
Whetting his knife for the cut he has missed
This time. Why do you gape. Enter the chamber.
There's feed for you. Look yourself sated with the
Painting I've seen, and not as the first one.
The hand that painted that, it was not blind.
Macbeth and Lenox exit.
Hey. Strike the bell.
SERVANT   Why, Sir, if you permit.
MACDUFF   Because I'll make a hole into your paunch else.
SERVANT   That's a good reason, Sir. Long live the King.
MACDUFF   What do you say. You know of whom you speak, man.
SERVANT   Of the King. The King's the King. And if
It is not him it is another one.
This or that one.
MACDUFF   This or that one. The dog
Got politics under his tongue. Shall I
Tear it out for you, man.
With the help of two Servants, who seize the man and force his jaws open,
Macduff cuts his tongue off. The Servant screams.
MACDUFF   That saves the bell. Hey, wake up Thanes. You hear

The meat calling for eaters. To dinner, butchers.
Murder has set the table, treason salted
The meat. Show me your hands: white is bloody.
Keep screaming, man. Shall I cut your throat.
Throw off your downy slumber, the ape of death
Take your seat between his teeth now and
Warm yourself in view of Judgment day
Arise like from your coffins now, and run
Like ghosts, racing with maggots for your flesh.
Lady Macbeth.
LADY MACBETH   What hideous trumpet is this. Has it been
Made in your workshop. Why do you disturb
The sleep of innocence.
MACDUFF   Oh gentle Lady
It's not for you to hear what I could tell
With my tongue and with that one.
Banquo.
Banquo.
The King has been murdered.
LADY MACBETH   In our house.
BANQUO   Cruel wherever. Say that you lie, Macduff.
Macbeth and Lenox.
MACBETH   Had I but died an hour before this
Blessed was my time here. After this today
What is still sacred between filth and blood.
All is but toys, glory is rank, grace putrid.
The wine has been filled into barrels, and
The lees still foam in the hollow press.
Malcolm. Donalbain.
MALCOLM and DONALBAIN   For whom is this moaning.
MACBETH   For you. Don't you know it.
Pause.

The source is plugged wherefrom your blood once sprung.
MACDUFF   The King, your father, has been murdered.
MALCOLM   By whom.
LENOX   His grooms have, if appearance doesn't lie,
Done the deed. Faces and hands were marked
With blood all over as if they had washed
Themselves in it. Their daggers were red too
We found them laid out on their pillows like
The proof of work deserving glory. Numb
With madness they were staring at us as if
All things alive would be thorns to their eye.
MACBETH   Had I but checked my fury. I have killed them.
MACDUFF   Why have you done that.
MACBETH   Who is in his horror
Wise, cold in his fury, sluggish with duty.
Too hurried was my love that stepped unto
My reason, which cried Halt. There he laid
His gray corpse embroidered with his blood,
And his gashed wounds looked like a breach in nature
For ruin's entrance. There his murderers
Painted with their trade, in sheaths of blood
Their daggers. Whoever has a heart to love
And courage in that heart to make love known,
Would then hold back his sword.
LADY MACBETH   Help me away.
MACDUFF   Look to the lady.
MALCOLM   Why do we hold our tongues
Brother, with the first claim to wail.
DONALBAIN   What I
Should bemoan cripples my tongue. This father's
Corpse goes pregnant, brother, with your death
And mine. Let us away before these tears

Will drown us, and before this pain will nail
Us to the floor here.
BANQUO   Look to the lady. When we
Have covered our too flimsy skins, Sirs,
That all too easy will make blush a sword
If they go naked, we will question this
Most bloody piece of work to know it further.
Between doubt and fear in the great hand of
God, I stand against silent suspicion.
MACDUFF   And so do I.
LENOX   So we are all in His hand
Who, if He likes to, bends the globe within
His fist.
MACBETH   I wish that He would like to do so.
Put on your irons and come to the hall.
Exeunt al except Malcolm and Donalbain.
MALCOLM   What will you do. It is not good to dine
With those mourners. We easily could be
The funeral banquet, brother. I'll go to England.
DONALBAIN   To Ireland I. Our separated fortune
Shall keep us both the safer. Where we are now
Daggers stare from every smile. The nearer
In blood the bloodier what's near.
MALCOLM   The shaft
That's shot is still in flight. We have no way but
Avoid its aim. Let's not be dainty, brother,
With taking leave. The manners have been changed here.
The moon snows blood.
Exeunt Malcolm and Donalbain. Servant.
SERVANT   The price of beer goes up.

10

The Peasant in the stock: a skeleton with shreds of flesh. Old Woman.
Young Peasant. Snow.

WOMAN   Give me back my husband.
What have you done to my husband. I'm not married to a bone. Why didn't
you pay the rent, blockhead. *Beats the corpse.*
YOUNG PEASANT *pulls her away:* With what. The dogs have been at him
already.
One hand is gone too. We will collect what's left before the dogs are through
with him.
They won't count his bones where he is going now. Don't cry. The snot is
freezing on your cheeks. If you'll be gone who is going to be my horse. A wife
I won't get with all that rent we owe. One has been killed, they say. The King.
You hear the horses. That's the smell of blood. We won't get him out of here
safe and sound. There's still too much flesh on him.
They duck down in the snow. Rosse. Macduff.
ROSSE   How does the world go, Sir .
MACDUFF   How. Don't you see it.
ROSSE   Who then has done this more than bloody deed.
MACDUFF   Those who can't deny it nor confess it.
Since Macbeth helped them step into their grave.
ROSSE   Why should they have slaughtered their golden goose.
MACDUFF   For more gold. Malcolm and Donalbain,
The sons of the dead majesty, have fled.
Only suspicion is what they have gained.
ROSSE   A miracle of nature: thriftless ambition!
So Scotland then belongs now to Macbeth.
MACDUFF   He is already named and goes to Scone for
The coronation.

ROSSE   You'll go to Scone, Sir, with the
New King.
MACDUFF   No, cousin, I'll go to Fyfe with me.
ROSSE   I'll go the other way.
MACDUFF   Do as you like. Adieu.
The old robe is gone now. Quick on your road
Take care the new one doesn't pinch your throat.
Exeunt in opposite directions. The Young Peasant and the Old Woman begin to
pick the dead body from the stocks.

11

Banquo.

BANQUO You have it: Glamis and Cawdor, King now.
As the weird women promised; and I fear
You played, that it came true, most fouly for it.
Yet they have also said: your tree-trunk, Macbeth,
Will have no branches. But that I should be
The root of many kings who follow you.
If there comes truth from our bearded sisters,
And on his head the ring does say it loudly,
Why should I not set me up in good hope.
Here comes a King who has no time. Already
My suns are rising through his skeleton.
Macbeth as King, Lady Macbeth as Queen. Rosse, Lenox, Lords.
MACBETH   Here's our chief guest.
LADY MACBETH   If he had been forgotten
It had been like a breach within our joys.
MACBETH   Tonight we hold a solemn supper, Sir.
And I'll request your presence.
BANQUO   Let Your Highness

Command upon me, to the which my duties
Are joined forever with a close knit bond.
MACBETH   You ride this afternoon.
BANQUO   I will, my lord.
MACBETH   We should have else desired your good advice
Which always has been grave and prosperous
In today's council. We'll hear you tomorrow.
Do you ride far.
BANQUO   'Twixt now and supper, Sir.
And if my horse won't make it, I must borrow
From the night.
MABETH   Don't miss our feast.
BANQUO   Not I, my lord.
MACBETH   We hear our bloody cousins are
In England and in Ireland, not confessing
Their cruel parricide, work at their hearers
With strange fairy-tales. But more of that
Tomorrow when we all meet for state business.
Sir, we release you to your horses now,
Till you return at night. Goes Fleance with you.
BANQUO   Ay, my lord. And our time is brief.
MACBETH   I wish you horses swift and sure of foot
And so do I commend you to their backs.
Farewell.
Exit Banquo.
And you be master of your time
Till tonight. That your society
Be sweeter for us, we will keep ourselves
Alone till supper time. God be with you!
Exeunt all but Macbeth.
I cannot need him now and here. Did I
Ever need him. If he could stop the time.

I can with no more than four hired hands.
Servant.
Servant.
The men called here to entertain us,
Are they at hand.
SERVANT At the gate, my Lord.
MACBETH   Bring them before us.
Exit Servant.
My fear is called Banquo.
He has too long been next to me, he can
Not be below me, nor above him I
On a safe chair. He also has one head
Too many since that heath. LESSER THAN
MACBETH AND MORE Banquo the kingmaker.
I want to shorten him his too steep member
Till maggots mate with him, and his brood too.
Upon my head is dry like straw the crown
And in my grip a scepter without fruit.
A stranger's hand will wrench it from my fist,
Dead or alive, because in my blood's tracks
No son will lift the boot, his seed be King.
To plough for him with swords this lewd and rank
Loam of human flesh. To turn the mill of
Power, crunching bones for his brood's bellies
That do wait now behind my carrion.
I will tear out future's genitals
If nothing comes of me, nothingness shall
Come of me. Who is coming there.
Enter Servant with Two Murderers.
Stay at the door until we're calling you.
Exit Servant.
Was it not yesterday we talked together.

MURDERER 1   Yesterday, majesty.

MURDERER 2   With your permission.

MACBETH   Have you considered what I told you. Know
That it was he, who kept you in times past
Lower than dogs, which you thought had been our
Innocent self's fault. He, Banquo.

MURDERER 1   You made it
Known to us.

MACBETH   What will you do about it.

MURDERER 2   My lord, whatever you want.

MACBETH   Do you savor
The muck that feeds his harvest. Are you men.

MURDERER 1   With your permission, my lord.

MACBETH   How now. Would you
Pray for this good man and his issue that
While alive will make you taste your grave
And mine.

MURDERER 1   We want to fold our hands, my lord,
Around his throat.

MACBETH   Are you strong prayers then.

MURDERER 1   The world has taught us how to pray, my lord.

MACBETH   So I impress this labor on your heart,
That will remove him and place you in our
Heart that suffers as long as he has his blood.
You pray for Scotland.

MURDERER 2   My lord, for what you want.
I am one whom the vile blows and the buffets
Of the world have so incensed that I no
More ask what I do to spite the world.

MURDERER 1   And I another, weary with disasters,
Wrenched by fortune, that I would put my life
On any chance, to mend or get rid of it.

MACBETH   And you know Banquo was your enemy
And mine, and in such bloody distance that
His breath is choking me.
MURDERER 1   We know, my lord.
MACBETH   With barefaced power I could sweep him from
My sight and my will would absolve me, yet
I must not, because certain friends are both
His and mine, whose loves I need to keep,
But bewail his fall must I, who killed him.
This is the reason why I'm wooing you
For your hand very talented with death
That you may lend it to me as a glove
Masking my grip, because the state demands it,
From the common eye.
MURDERER 2   We shall, my lord,
Perform what you command us.
MURDERER 1   With every throat,
You are so gracious to entrust to us.
MACBETH   Through your dull nature shines nobility.
Still in this hour I'll advise you where
To plant yourselves; the time and the best moment;
For tonight it must be done; and far from
The palace, not to smear my innocence.
And with him, so of your work is no trace left
Fleance his son, who keeps him company,
Must share the fate of your deadly embrace,
Out of the sun for us. You're ready.
MURDERERS   We are.
MACBETH   Go hide yourself and wait until the hour.
Exeunt Murderers.
That was Banquo. The rest is for the dogs.
Lady Macbeth.

LADY MACBETH

Why alone, majesty. The crown too heavy.

Let me help you carry it. Don't bury

Yourself in sorry fancies, and continue

Thoughts of the kind that should indeed have died

With him you think of. What one cannot change

One shouldn't think of. Done is done. —Banquo

Is gone from court?

MACBETH   And will return.

LADY MACBETH   Whereto.

MACBETH   From where he left.

LADY MACBETH   Like all that's living. When.

MACBETH   Life is a race that is aiming at death.

LADY MACBETH   Comb sleek your face, my lord and King. Be bright

And jovial among your guests tonight.

MACBETH   I will, my love. And you shall too, with him

Above all others, Banquo. Full of scorpions

Is my mind, dear wife, and in this night

They are afoot. Unsafe the throne. With our

Spittle we have to rinse our power and

Make our faces masks of our hearts.

Your smile tonight should belong to him, Banquo.

We've notched the serpent but we failed to kill it.

She grows together and is new as she was

And threatened by her fang again lives our

Poor malice. Let the frame of things disjoint

In this or yonder world ere we will eat

The sweat of our fears and go to sleep

In the embrace of these horrible dreams

That choke us nightly. Better dead with the dead

Whom we've tread down to step up to his place

Than lie stretched out upon the torture bench

With all our nerves. Duncan is in his grave.
It's our treason that has helped him out of
The fevers of this life. He sleeps well.
Poison, steel, rebellion, war, nothing
Can touch him now. Your best smile tonight
For Banquo.
LADY MACBETH   What do you want to do.
MACBETH   Don't worry
About that. Your smile for Banquo.
LADY MACBETH   Could I but
Smile him to his death.
MACBETH   It's men, woman,
That this world has been made by and it's only
Men that can shake its structure to the core.
Go and be beautiful for our guests.
LADY MACBETH   Would I be it for you still.
MACBETH   My bride's called Scotland.
LADY MACBETH   *bares her breasts:*
The one who made that bed for you was I, Sir.
MACBETH   Cover yourself, Lady, power is cold.
LADY MACBETH   And you'll scream for my breasts when all is told.
Exit Lady Macbeth

12

Three Murderers.

MURDERER 1   Who did bid you to join hands with us.
MURDERER 3   MACBETH.
MURDERER 1   Your earnest.
Murderer 3 shows the money.
MURDERER 2   What riches in such rags.

We trust you, comrade.

MURDERER 1   Here is the proof.

Rams his knife into the back of Murderer 3.

Comrade.

Pockets the money.

What do you want.

MURDERER 2   My share.

MURDERER 1   Have you made him

Mute.

MURDERER 2   No, Banquo, "our enemy." *They laugh.*

MURDERER   Here.

Gives him some of the dead man's money.

We'll put him down here as a signpost.

We can get easier at those gentlemen

When they stoop down for the fresh carrion.

An honest man: even when dead he works

For his earnest.

MURDERER 2   The night now crams the day

Into its teeth.

MURDERER 1   Tomorrow it will spit us

The next one in the face. And this today

Is yesterday's vomit.

MURDERER 2   I wish I had

Something between my teeth now.

MURDERER 1   There comes your meat.

You hear the horses. All goes as we planned.

The gentlemen leave to the serfs their stable

And walk the straight way to here through the wood.

For love of nature or whatever.

MURDERER 2   Maybe, they have some inkling of the assault

And have their monkeys dangle from the swing.

MURDERER 1   Well, nothing ever beats a clever nose.

MURDERER 2   They're in a hurry to fill their bellies.

MURDERER 1   Ours.

Banquo and Fleance, with torches.

BANQUO   What lies here in the way. Another horror.

FLEANCE   Something in rags. Nothing to stoop for.

BANQUO   There will be rain tonight.

MURDERER 1   On you.

BANQUO   Run, son.

Live for vengeance.

MURDERER 1 *cuts his throat:*

He's got it over with.

Fleance frees himself from the hands of Murderer 2, escapes.

MURDERER 1   Where is the other one. You let him go.

MURDERER 2 *holding his arm:* That lousy rat has bitten my wrist.

MURDERER 1   He was the better half of our labor.

MURDERER 2   How can I do my labor with that bone.

MURDERER 1   What do I know. Let's go and tell what's done.

Wait.

Cuts off BANQUO's penis.

A love-token for our master.

The root of evil.

MURDERER 2   He won't get up no more. *Laughs.*

13

Banquet. Macbeth, Lady Macbeth, Lords and Servants.

MACBETH   You know yourself your rank.

Take now your seats.

LORDS   Thanks to your Majesty. *Silent struggle for the seats.*

MACBETH   We ourselves will

Mingle with society and play

The humble host. The ruler of our heart
Will grace the throne. To open our feast
She'll say the welcome.
LADY MACBETH Say it for me, Sir,
To all. For all are welcome, says my heart.
MACBETH And from their heart they all are thanking you.
My place be in the midst of you.
Lords are competing to offer him their seats.
Bring wine.
Murderer 1.
There's blood upon your face.
MURDERER 1 It's Banquo's then.
MACBETH Better upon you than in him. He's gone.
MURDERER 1 *flapping his arms like wings:*
Well on his way, my lord. And the rain pours
Down his throat. That is what I did for him.
MACBETH You are the best of cutthroats. Good is too
Who did the like for Fleance. If you did it
There is none better than you.
MURDERER 1 My lord, that fish
Was too small for our net. He slipped the mesh.
MACBETH Again there reaches for my crown just any
Wind over Scotland. Would I be made of marble
I could dress myself in my monument,
Like Duncan who is dead. They gulp my wine down,
Pressed from their peasants, and my saliva
And all is but a foretaste of my blood. —
Drink, friends. This Banquo, is he gone for good.
MURDERER 1
Sir, like this tube that propagated him.
MACBETH You're mocking me. Man, who has prompted you.
MURDERER 1 Each trade has its own humor, my king.

MACBETH   The serpent is gone. Thanks for it. The escaped
Worm has from his birth venom time will ripen,
But no tooth for the present. Go. And bring
This toy here to your children. Have you children.
You carry their life on your tongue. Be silent.
More tomorrow.
Exit Murderer 1.
LADY MACBETH   My most royal lord,
With their filled cheeks our guests are starving for
Your favor. If it lacks, the meat lacks flavor.
MACBETH   Beloved admonisher. May to your stomachs
Friends, be pleasant, what your palate loved.
LENOX   May it please Your Highness, to take your seat.
Banquo's Ghost on Macbeth's seat.
MACBETH   Here under one roof would be Scotland's nobles
Were the priced person of our Banquo present;
Whom I may rather scold for being cold
Than pity for mishap.
ROSSE   His absence, Sir,
Lays blame upon his promise. Please it, your Highness,
To grace us with your royal company.
MACBETH   The table's occupied.
LENOX   Here is your place, Sir.
MACBETH   My place. Where.
LENOX   Here, in our midst, Sir.
MACBETH   Who of you did this.
LORDS   What displeases you, Sir.
MACBETH   What would please me, if my eyes didn't see it.
You love to see me thus, don't you.
LORDS   Sir, our duty—
MACBETH   You cannot say I did it. I did not.
Not that with my own hand. Never shake that

Helmet at me, knitted from your spilled blood.
No more will you exchange that for my crown.
Go join the maggots. There wait for me, friend.
ROSSE   Gentlemen, rise. His Highness is not well.
LADY MACBETH   Stay, worthy friends. The King is often thus
And has been from his youth. Pray, keep your seat.
The fit is momentary. Upon one thought
He is again himself. If much you note him
You shall offend him and extend his pain.
Eat, and regard him not. —Are you a man.
MACBETH   And a bold one, that dares looking at
What might appall the devil. You see the corpse
That sits astride my chair. Your smile for Banquo.
LADY MACBETH   Oh proper stuff! The painting of your fear.
The air-drawn dagger that led you to Duncan.
Much wind about the after-birth of horror.
Why fear what has been out of fear now, his one
And ours. A women's story at a winter's
Fire is what shakes you. Shame on you.
Making faces at an empty chair.
MACBETH   What do you want. We all step over corpses
Throughout our life. Shall I hack off your flesh
From your bones and throw it to the dogs.
If our gravesites won't hold those we bury
Behind us, may the maws of vultures be our
Final hole.
LADY MACBETH   Quite unmanned in folly.
MACBETH   I saw him. Blood has been shed before,
Ere the law built the state's skeleton;
And since then murders without name and number
Have been performed. It always was so: when
The brains were out, the man would die, and nothing

Came after. But now the dead do rise again,
The skull with twenty holes the wind blows through
And rain rains in, yet they do rise again,
And push us from our chairs, or take their seat
On our back to ride into the ground
Our majesty.
LADY MACBETH   My king, your friends miss you.
MACBETH   As we are lacking Banquo, our friend.
Bring wine. More of it. To the table's health!
And Banquo's! Bring on fresh meat. Eat, my friends!
What stuffs your stomachs, cannot bite you later.
Gulp it down faster, you, the dead grow fast
Fattening their yesterdays with our mornings.
Could I devour all meat of the world
With such a hunger that it won't rise again.
What do you stare at, comrade. With eyes that
Are not yours anymore. The property
Of crows they are. Go. There's no blood left in
Your veins that the rain is washing now.
Alone now with your bones you will be soon,
Your shirt the earth. Go, carrion, or put on your
Flesh again and dare me, sword against sword,
Into the desert.
LADY MACBETH   The worry for the state does
Curtail his sleep. The yoke of Kings, my lords.
LENOX   Sir, our loyalty—
ROSSE   Trust us, my king.
MACBETH   What can you do against the spirits. Trust you.
Who are you. Strange to myself you make me
Watching my bloody sights like they are nothing.
Are you of their stuff then, a gateway for
Fear and death.

ROSSE   What kind of sights, my lord.

MACBETH   I will force open your eyes with my sword.

LADY MACBETH *steps in front of his sword:*

Go now. Don't ask. Good night to all of you.

Stand not upon your rank when you are going,

But go at once.

LENOX   We wish you a good sleep, highness.

Exeunt quickly the Lords.

MACBETH   Are they gone.

LADY MACBETH   Yes.

MACBETH   Blood will have blood, they say.

Stones have been known to move and trees to speak;

Against the murderer. That are all lies.

Is it still night.

LADY MACBETH   It is at odds with morning.

MACBETH   Banquo came right on time at our bidding.

He wanted back his blood, or did he not.

I'll pour him other blood. That juice is cheap.

What do you say, Macduff rejects our love.

There is not one in who's house I don't keep

A servant who is my ear, paid by me.

The witches, my bearded sisters, I wanted

To ask them yesterday, on that same heath.

But they did not appear. Wherever they are

Housed in this Scotland, I shall go and find them

And if I have to turn its ground top under,

Or with my nails I dig them from its rock

And question them. For I do need to know

All there is to know. All shall be building

Stones of my fortune. I have stepped so deep

Now into blood that, should I wade no more,

Returning were as tedious as to go on.

There are things in my head that grab my hand,
Which rather must be acted on than scanned.
LADY MACBETH   You lack what shelters our life from death,
Sleep. Come to bed.
MACBETH   My craze and self-abuse
Is the initiate's fear that lacks hard use.
We are yet young in butchery.

14

Stone slabs move across the stage, carried by crawling peasants. Two Figures.

FIGURE 1   Doomsday is upon us. The stones are walking
FIGURE 2   To Dunsinane. Scotland's King is building
A castle against Scotland.

15

Lenox. Lord.

LENOX   I say what is. Think what you want about it.
In strange ways one stone fits the other one.
I say no more. The gracious Duncan is
Pitied by Macbeth. Well, he was dead.
The right valiant Banquo walked out late;
Whom, you can say, if you want, Fleance killed,
For Fleance fled. Men must not walk too late.
Not if you have a son. And who could think
Otherwise than with repugnance of
Malcolm and Donalbain. To have butchered
Their snow-white father. What a hateful deed.
How Macbeth was distraught. Did he not straight

In pious rage hack dead the two delinquents
Who were still enchained by drink and sleep.
Was not that nobly done. And wisely too.
Would any beating heart not be enraged
By their shameless denial. So that, I say
Macbeth has turned well all things with his born
Majesty. I think had he in his grasp
Duncan's sons and Fleance, son of Banquo,
On the same school bench they would learn what it
Means to kill the father out of love
For the state's treasury. Since now they fill it
Having fled their bloodied legacy.
Is that not strange. And also to the best has
Macbeth turned this, our most gracious lord.
Has he not eased the rent our peasants pay us
That was so badly squashing our stomachs.
Has he not for their long time loyalty,
To Duncan and to him, richly rewarded
His army. And how frugal he himself lives:
The horses in his stable, they say, feed on
Horse meat since that night when under his roof
Duncan laid there in his blood, and two of
His horses broke their stalls, and attacked wildly
Each other, rudely tore apart with hooves
And teeth and, quite as humans do, devoured
Off the bone each one the other's flesh.
LORD   I've heard of it.
LENOX   What do you hear of Macduff,
Who was your friend.
LORD   Not mine, Sir, since he staid
Away from the banquet with "Sir, not I"
And wants to make his way to England where

56

Malcolm, as one hears—

LENOX   I hear it from you.

LORD   Is favored by that pious Edward and

Boasts of his due of birth, and brags about

How, with heaven's protection and with England's

Army, he'll see to it we may again

Give our tables meat, sleep our nights,

Freedom to our feasts from barefaced lies

And bloody knives, for which we all yearn now.

Must I say more.

LENOX   You see me shocked, Sir.

Pause.

The heaven over Scotland tastes of smoke.

LORD   Yes, of certain castles.

LENOX   And villages

That may well serve as torches for the fire.

LORD   For Scotland there's no peasant too good for me.

LENOX   And for its King I throw Scotland away.

16

Dunsinane. Macbeth is drinking.

MACBETH   Hail Macbeth. Hail. King of Scotland Hail!

He laughs, until the crown falls from his head. It rolls across the floor, he crawls after it and catches it with the scepter. He throws it into the air, catches it again with the scepter, whirls it around, and so forth.

A Messenger.

MESSENGER   News from England, Sir, Macduff and Malcolm

Collect an army from the dregs of harbors

To war for Scotland's crown.

Exit. Macbeth puts the crown on his head.

MACBETH   That boy Malcolm.

Macduff, whom I outspit with regicide
My best enemy I forgot to butcher.
What is that sound. The queen screams in her sleep.
You should then sleep no more, my queen. You could
Scream out what makes you screaming in your sleep.
MACBETH IS MURDERING SLEEP.
Laughs.
THE SLEEP THAT HAS
NO GUILT. My fear was called Banquo. But I
Have written down his name into the dust.
The dead will not come back to Dunsinane.
The wings of angels do not carry that far.
My throne-room no more won't contain their number
And no more lonesome they rot in abundance.
I gave the dead more dead as company.
Laughs.
HAIL BANQUO, LESSER THAN MACBETH AND MORE
WITCHES.
WITCHES   Hail Macbeth. Hail! King of Scotland, Hail!
MACBETH   You. I have searched for you on our heath.
WITCH 1   We graze on all of Scotland's bloody meadows.
MACBETH   You come up very high to Dunsinane.
WITCH 2   To see you at the summit of your fortune.
WITCH 3   And presents are we bringing for your table.
WITCH 1   A newborn's little hand. It is still fresh.
His mother choked it only yesterday
Between her thighs. Herself she lies chopped up by
The executioner now.
WITCH 2   A dog's stomach
Through which a peasant passed some days ago.
WITCH 3   A royal banner made of human skin
For Dunsinane, firmly built on bones.

Macbeth throws over the table with the witches' presents:
Why should the ground I walk on bother me.
Laughter of the Witches. The hall is rocking. Macbeth falls down.
On his hands and knees. What it looks down there I'll learn soon enough
I want to know: how will I stay on top.
How will go Malcolm's war and Banquo's brood.
I gave you blood to quaff. Do you want more.
Answer me. All Scotland's graveyards full of
Corpses for one view into time's bowels.
The Witches ride on him, tear out his hair and his clothes into tatters, fart into
his face, and so forth. Finally they let him lie there, half naked, and screeching
throw the crown to each other; until one of them puts it on her head. A fight for
the crown with teeth and claws, while a GRAND VOICE speaks the following
text.
GRAND VOICE   Salve yourself with blood, do as you like and slaughter
Man is but filth, his life is just a laughter
Because no one who woman gave birth to
Is going to attain that death takes you
Be invincible until trees will reign
And Birnam's wood will march to Dunsinane.
The Witches vanish. Macbeth, naked on his belly, crawls towards the crown,
collects the tatters of his clothes, and so forth.
MACBETH   Nail to the cross of winds Scotland's churches
Crush their steeples deep into the dust
And heap on Scotland's nobles all their castles.
Let my breakers swallow down my ships
And with my peasants' bodies dung my loam.
What do I fear. What's left for me to fear.
NO ONE BORN BY A WIFE, BIRNAM'S WOOD.
Puts the crown on his head.
Come, Malcolm and Macduff, into my spears.
By wives you have been screamed into the world

From bloody cunt on your way to the butcher.
Who puts under the yoke the wood commanding
The trees. Not until Birnam's wood does march
Has members the rebellion. My time is full.
Safe to the last leap, Macbeth will walk through
The dance of knives that is life, threatened by
No one but death that is innate to humans.
That makes me sweat nude in the freeze of dawn.
My heart is beating at my ribs, each beat
A death. Can you not count more softly, clockwork.
One moment. One more moment. And again.
That booms like drumming and I am the drum skin.
Must I hear this forever. Were I but deaf.
Do I still hear it. What dies no more is dead.
My life will be no longer than my dying.
It beats too fast. Can you not keep the pace.
It beats no more. Yes, all is still. Live on
Rebellious flesh. My scepter. And my crown.
I am Macbeth, the King, and I command
The death in Scotland. What is choking my throat.
The walls are closing in around my breast.
How shall I breathe within this shirt of stone.
Pause.
My grave yawned open one brief moment long.
Upon my tongue there was a taste of iron.
My flesh smells rotten. Am I who I am.
A dog's stomach would not smell too bad for me
If it offered a loophole from my grave.
Could I go back into the child I was.
I want to put on the skins of my dead ones,
To dress with rottenness my feeble flesh
And outlast myself in the mask of death.

I want to multiply the angels' army,
A wall of corpses to ward off my death.
You have a wife, Macduff. And have a child.
Macduff, you have a wife and child no more.
Soldiers.

17

Lady Macduff with Child. Macbeth with two Soldiers.

LADY MACDUFF What faces are these.
MACBETH   Others you'll see no more.
The Soldiers kill the child.
Have you hatched only one egg, Lady.
You would have more to butcher. Now it's you.
Exit Lady Macduff. The Soldiers follow her. We hear her scream.
Macbeth stays on stage, until the screaming ends.

18

Soldiers drag a shackled Lord before Macbeth.

SOLDIER   Here is the traitor, Sir. There burns his castle.
MACBETH   Who has commanded that you burn his castle.
SOLDIERS   We could not otherwise, Sir, get at him.
MACBETH   So pick now from the ashes too your loot,
How do you want to pay, Lord, for your treason.
LORD   The way you shall pay when it is your time.
LENOX   With his head, Sir, like all other traitors.
MACBETH   We're making war for raven's fodder, don't we.
Our army is feeding Scotland's maggots.
He was your friend, no.

LENOX   Till he betrayed you, Sir.

MACBETH   What makes you eager for his head. Your love

For Scotland, or fear that he could betray more

Than Scotland.

LENOX   Sir, with my own sword I want to.

MACBETH   Do you. Well, I shall not insist on proofs

As long as fear maintains your loyalty. —

Your estate's ashes will not wash you white.

LORD   And your ash will not wash the blood away

That you wade in. Can you swim, bloodhound.

MACBETH   He's got philosophy. That's perfect. Would you

Become my jester and, led by the leash,

Walk on four legs and rant against me, Lord

When we're alone. We do lack entertainment

At Dunsinane. There's little new of it

In our sky. And it gets less. Would you, Lord.

Soldiers laugh. Lord spits into Macbeth's face.

Pause.

He wants to give me back my spittle now

That he has guzzled at my banquet table

Lenox and Rosse wipe the spittle off his face.

With you, when he was still honest, as you are.

He is it still, an honest traitor, who

Pays his bill before he steps into his grave.

Soldiers laugh.

The payment, though, will not wash off your treason

Nor me the blood, of others and of yours

That soon you'll vomit into your own face.

SOLDIERS   We shall teach him, Sir, to walk at the leash and

On his four legs. Can you dance, my Lord.

Soldiers, holding the Lord by a rope, prod him with their spears and make him

dance.

Where is the widow. She shall see him dance
Other Soldiers bring the Lady.
ROSSE   I beg you, Sir, don't let the lady too
Serve for the rabble's lust, that makes today
The horse for this one and tomorrow that one.
MACBETH   You like her. Well, then take her. Share her
With Lenox, who is your friend and mine, too.
To the Soldiers:
What you may fish now from the castle's ruins
That gold is going to the crown. It needs it
To arm us against England.
Pointing at the Lord: That there is yours.
SOLDIERS   What shall we do with him.
MACBETH   What you want.
SOLDIER 1, *to the PRISONER:*
Sir, do you want to be King.
SOLDIER 2, *on his hands and knees:*
Your throne, majesty.
SOLDIER 3, *crams a helmet full of earth on the PRISONER's head:*
Here's your crown
SOLDIER 1   He doesn't want to be King.
SOLDIER 2, *throws off the Prisoner:* He's not anointed yet.
Soldiers drag the Prisoner with the rope across the ground.
ROSSE   They make fun
Of Scotland's majesty.
MACBETH   It entertains me.
It also entertains my soldiers here.
Do you begrudge us, Sir, the entertainment.
SOLDIER 4   Let me. We have some old business, the lord
And I. My father died due to the rent he
Owed, my lord, and as his loyal son
I want to settle his bill. And not till

63

You look the same way as my father looked
When your dogs had been finished with him as
They tore him apart, Sir, in your courtyard,
A show to please your ladies, we'll be quits, Sir.
And for your lady I'll perform the show now.
SOLDIER 1   I am game.
SOLDIER 2   I always liked to know
What underneath his pelt a lord looks like.
SOLDIER 3   Maybe we'll find there what made him a lord.
SOLDIER 1   We want to strip him bare down to his soul.
The Soldiers are skinning the Prisoner.
MACBETH *watching:* As if they had been reading Ovid: "WHY
DO YOU PULL ME OUT OF MYSELF. SCREAMED MARSYAS
BUT WHILE HE SCREAMED THE GOD PULLED THE SKIN
FROM HIS MEMBERS HE WAS ONE SINGLE WOUND
TO EYES VISIBLE THE NETWORK OF MUSCLES
THE TUBING OF THE VEINS WAS ALL EXPOSED
AND WITH YOUR HANDS YOU COULD GRAB HIS ENTRAILS."
Why do you bawl, woman. The clergy lies.
You are not both One Body.
ROSSE *softly:* Marsyas was
A peasant.
MACBETH *laughs:* Well, the times they are a changing.
At the charred portal of the castle is hanging, head down, the slaughtered Lord of the castle.
SOLDIER 4   You recognize again the peasant, Lady,
Who has gone to school and taught by your dogs.
ROSSE and LENOX   That is rebellion.
MACBETH   Yes. The ice is thin
Where on we're roasting our peasants. Help
Us to keep the throne, so the throne keeps you.
Soldiers. Do you love your King.

SOLDIERS   Hail
Macbeth, King of Scotland.
MACBETH *points at SOLDIER 4:* Cut him down.
A long silence. Then the Soldiers execute the command.

19

Physician. Lady- In-Waiting.

PHYSICIAN   You have seen how she walked in her sleep.
LADY-IN-WAITING   Yes
And how she washed her hands in empty air.
And who saw it before me is seen no more.
PHYSICIAN   A rare disturbance of nature: asleep
Going around and wash the hands with air.
What did you hear her say out of her sleep.
LADY-IN-WAITING   What I will not report after her, Sir.
PHYSICIAN   You may trust the physician. You should, lady.
LADY-IN-WAITING   Neither you nor others. With no witness
Sir, to confirm my words. —There she comes.
Lady Macbeth.
PHYSICIAN   With her eyes open.
LADY-IN-WAITING   Yes, but she cannot see.
PHYSICIAN   The heart it is a roomy graveyard.
LADY-IN-WAITING   Look.
LADY MACBETH   Another spot. Again. As if it grows back.
PHYSICIAN   She speaks. I will note down what she is saying .
LADY MACBETH   Away now, dirt. Wash your hands, my dear.
There rings the bell. The time, Sir, to do it.
How now, a soldier and afraid. Who knows it.
What do we fear, when our power is law.
Who would have thought that you have so much blood

In you, old man.

LADY-IN-WAITING Are you writing, Sir.

LADY MACBETH Macduff had a wife. And has no child now.

What, will these hands never be white again.

No more of that. It is a chair, that's it.

You cannot come back from the grave again

Say I. It still is smelling of the blood here.

For whom, Sir, is that dagger in your hand.

Exit.

LADY-IN-WAITING Have you been gone out of ink now, Sir.

PHYSICIAN This case is not within my practice, Lady.

I also have known some who walked asleep

And who then died in bed, blessed by God.

LADY-IN-WAITING We are at war with England, Sir. Keep writing.

PHYSICIAN Not I, Lady. We are at war with England.

He swallows what he has written.

20

Lenox and Rosse, with Soldiers, from opposite sides.

ROSSE Whereto, Lord.

LENOX Where there is victory.

ROSSE Here is the way to Dunsinane.

LENOX My way to

Dunsinane goes by the way of Birnam.

ROSSE Where England's forces are.

LENOX And Scotland's King.

ROSSE Sir, that is treason.

The Soldiers take positions fronting each other.

LENOX Against whom. What is

More to your taste then, Lord.

To Rosse's Soldiers: And to yours:
Scottish dust or English ale.
SOLDIERS To Birnam.

21

Macbeth. Physician. Messengers.

MACBETH   Save me your reports. Let all of them flee.
Till Birnam's wood will march to Dunsinane.
No fear can taint me. Who is Malcolm. A boy.
Born by woman, whom the whores of London
Painted with cheek that may be thought as nerve
In their bed sheets' sweat. Run, lords, ahead
Of your peasants just to lick his spittle,
Of mine you've long enough nourished yourselves
And creep under the women skirts of England.
The crown has grown fixed to my skull by now,
And my heart that I carry here does not beat
Faster than it did the very first day.
Messenger.
The devil burn you black. You milk-faced boy.
Wherefrom did you get that goose look, kid.
MESSENGER   There are ten thousand—
MACBBETH   Geese.
MESSENGER   Soldiers, Sir.
MACBETH   Go prick your face, clown, and paint your fear red
Before I let them cut a new face for you
You lily-white liver. Which soldiers, dog.
Death on your soul. That corpses' sheet that hangs
Beneath your helmet, it is spreading fear.
You want to dangle in the sun for drying.

What sort of soldiers, milk face.

MESSENGER Sir, the forces

Of England, Sir, with your permission. And, Sir—

MACBETH Take your face out.

Exit Messenger.

Seyton! —My stomach strikes

When I see my people. Seyton. This war

Links me with chains to the throne of Scotland

Or topples me. I lived long enough

My way went to the desert, under my boot

Dry leaves still rustle. What is due to old age,

Honors and love, obedience, the troops

Of friends, it leaves me out. My shares are

Backhanded curses whispered in my rear,

As long as daggers are too short still, now

I see them grow. Mouth-honor and, out of

Fear of my daggers, loyal service which

That poor pack would deny but does not dare to.

Seyton.

Seyton.

SEYTON What is your pleasure, Sir.

MACBETH What news.

SEYTON All has been confirmed.

MACBETH Give me my armor.

We shall fight until from my bones my flesh

Has been hacked off.

SEYTON It is not yet the time, Sir.

MACBETH Send out more soldiers. Strip all of Scotland bare.

Hang those that bleat of fear. Give me my armor.

How does your patient, doctor.

DOCTOR Not so sick

My Lord, as troubled with perplexing fancies

She walks with while asleep.

MACBETH   Cure her of that.

Can you not help a mind that is unwell

Pluck from the memory a rooted pain

Raze out what troubles wrote into a brain.

Have you no means to shovel free the breast of

The load that weighs upon the heart, a sweet

Forgetting.

DOCTOR   Therein the patient must be

His own doctor.

MACBETH   Throw your art to the dogs,

But not to me. Help me into my armor.

My spear. Seyton, send horsemen out. Doctor

My thanes run from me. Get going. Could you

Doctor, draw from my land the water. I have

Bled it long enough, could you find its

Disease and purge that badly flogged body

To pristine health, I surely would applaud you

And the echo of it applaud you too.

Pull off that strap, man, if it does not hold.

A hole in my armor is not what I fear.

Have you no purgative against England,

Doctor. Give me my helmet. Take the crown.

You want to have it. What do you fear most, Seyton.

SEYTON   An empty purse.

MACBETH   Here is a full one. Put it

On my grave stone when it is empty.

SEYTON   Sir,

I hope you will survive it.

MACBETH   Hey, do you

Love your king, Seyton.

SEYTON   No, my lord.

MACBETH   And why do you want that I live, Seyton.

SEYTON   Because to England's dogs we are the same flesh.

MACBETH   If you will stick that spear into my back
We will be no more.

SEYTON   Yes, Sir.

MACBETH *hands him his spear:* Bear that for me.
Exit, with his back to Seyton, who follows him.

DOCTOR   It smells of death at Dunsinane. I came
Here for profit. Were I still poor.
A Maid runs across the stage. Madam.
Have you a bed for me.
Exit, following the Maid.

22

Soldiers are chasing a Peasant. The Peasant falls down.

SOLDIER 1 *bending over the Peasant:* Why do you run away, peasant, from
the king's soldiers. *Threatens him with his weapon.* Are you afraid.

PEASANT   Yes, Sir.

SOLDIER 2   He is afraid. That's the rope, peasant.

PEASANT *desperate:* Long live the King.

SOLDIER 1   Which king, knave.

PEASANT   The one of Scotland.

SOLDIER 2 *slyly:* Do you know his name.

PEASANT *after a pause, relieved:* Duncan, Sir.

SOLDIER 1   That's the rope again. We'll have to hang you twice. Macbeth
is the name of our gracious king and warlord, who gives you this rope as
a present, peasant, so that you learn how to fly. Remember his name for
eternity.

The Peasant prays.

SOLDIER 2 *puts the rope around his neck:* Amen.

English Soldiers enter, drive the Scottish Soldiers into flight and exeunt, in

their pursuit. The Peasant pulls his head from the noose and wants to run away.
The English Soldiers return and catch him.
PEASANT   *in a panic:* Hail Macbeth, King of Scotland.
ENGLISH SOLDIER   That was your last hail. We are going to hang you,
dog, for that name, as an enemy of Scotland.
They put the noose again around his neck. Scottish Soldiers enter, drive the
English Soldiers into flight and exeunt, in their pursuit. The Peasant pulls his
head from the noose and remains sitting on the ground.
PEASANT   I'm going to hang myself before the soldiers come back, the
one kind or the others. The world is moving too fast for my poor head. At
least I won't suffer very long, it is a good rope.
He puts the noose again around his neck. Come, dear lord Jesus.

23

Macbeth, Seyton, Soldiers.
Shouts: They're coming!
MACBETH   Hang out our banner on the outward walls.
Exeunt Soldiers.
That screams. What do they fear. As if their lives
Were not enough like death. Go, stop that screaming.
Soldiers exeunt. Sound of beatings. Silence.
They come. Our castle here is Scotland's peak.
Let Malcolm exercise his milk tooth at it.
And my lords who once have piled them up with
Their peasants' hands, let them scratch at my stones
With their claws that I let them grow too long
And let them camp outside until they bite
Each other and their famine will eat all
Of them and plague will rot their flesh. We'd have
Torn off their beards from their faces and
Beat them back to England, one by one.

What is that noise.

SEYTON   The cries of women, Sir.

Exit.

MACBETH   I have forgotten how my sweat of fear tastes.

There was a time when night-shrieks made me shiver

Hearing a tale of terror made my hair raise

As if alive. I've crammed myself with horrors

And ghouls were close to my butcher's brain.

Seyton.

SEYTON   Why that Scream.

SEYTON   The queen is dead, Sir.

MACBETH   She could have died hereafter. Or before

When there was time for a word that means nothing.

Have you something to mourn for, Seyton.

SEYTON   No.

MACBETH   I wish you could lend me some pain that I

Would know that my heart is alive. Seyton, why

Do you not betray me.

SEYTON   Why should I.

MACBETH   Yes. —

Tomorrow and tomorrow and tomorrow

Creeps with its petty pace from day to day to

The last syllable. The rest is out of time.

All our yesterdays, led by blind men

Into dusty nothing. Do you know

Something else, Seyton. Out, out brief candle.

Life's but a walking shadow, a poor player

That struts and frets his hour on his stage

And then is heard no more. It is a tale

Told by an idiot, full of sound and fury

Signifying nothing.

A VOICE *sings:*

They took off their silken robe
And stuffed with it the hole
In their good ship's wooden lobe
The sea still took them whole.
MACBETH   They lust as if a copulation for
Death.
SEYTON   For yours, Sir.
MACBETH   Like I do too.
We'll pull the helmets lower on the face
When night does fall, Seyton. And no more stars.
A Messenger.
You've got something on the tongue. Spit it out.
MESSENGER   I must report that, which I say, I saw
And don't know how to tell it.
MACBETH   Say it, man.
MESSENGER   I was standing my watch upon that hill
And looked toward Birnam and then me thought
The wood began to walk.
MACBETH   You're lying slave.
MESSENGER   I will endure your wrath if it be not so.
As wide as three miles you can see it coming.
That wood is good at foot, Sir.
MACBETH   If you speak false
From the next tree you shall hang alive
Till famine clings you. If your speech is true
I care not if you do the same to me.
Another Messenger.
MESSENGER 2   The wood, Sir.
MACBETH   That's all you have to report.
What happened else but that a wood is marching.
Exeunt quickly the Messengers.
Why in such hurry. My place is the tree.

My pluck is drawing water, Seyton. My shield.
Damn the bearded women. FEAR NOT TILL
BIRNAM WOOD WILL MARCH TO DUNSINANE.
How they lied while they said the truth.
Take some soldiers, Seyton, and cut down
Who lifts a foot to flee. The women too.
And plant the corpses on the ramparts. We want
To make the wood fear us, pale its green.
SEYTON   The lady too, my lord.
MACBETH   What kind of lady.
Dead is dead. Seyton, throw torches at the wood.
I want to see, if the ashes stop marching.
Exit Seyton. Noise of battle. Glare of fire.
Get out of my face, sun! I have grown tired
To look at you. Were I but your grave, world.
Why shall I end now and you not at all.
Seyton, wounded.
SEYTON   The wood now burns, and up to Dunsinane
Climbs what has crawled from underneath its ashes
England's army and the Scottish army.
MACBETH   My army—
SEYTON   Opens the enemy the gates
I am your army now.
MACBETH   Go find a hole
In the castle wall. What do you wait for.
SEYTON   For nothing, Sir.
MACBETH   Don't you want to live.
SEYTON   Sir, it bores me.
Dies.
MACBETH   They tied me to a stake.
What can the bear do. Just wait for the dogs.
Shall I now play the Roman and thus eat

74

My sword.

Soldiers, some of them in ashes and burned clothes.

Here are other lives, their wounds fit

Better their face. Come on, all of you there!

Macbeth kills a Soldier, who is attacking him.

Where is he who has not been born by woman.

Soldiers surround Macbeth, until he stands in the center of a circle formed by the tips of their spears. The circle gets tighter. Macduff.

MACDUFF   Look around, bloodhound. No mother's body

Made as many sons as stand here to

Finally demand your blood from you.

MACBETH   Heaven and hell have jaws in their face.

My death won't make your world a better place.

The Soldiers ram their spears into his body, they pillage the corpse.

MACDUFF   The head goes to the crown.

A Soldier brings Macbeth's head on a spear

MALCOLM, ROSSE and LENOX   Hail Malcolm, King

Of Scotland. See how high he once has climbed

Who was it before you. Learn from his case.

MALCOLM   Know, you can't fool around with the boy Malcolm.

For your head is a place here on my spear.

Malcolm laughs. Rosse and Lenox point at Macduff.

Soldiers kill him.

MALCOLM   Have I said I want it. Were I in England.

Malcolm weeps. Soldiers put the crown on his head.

Witches.

WITCHES   Hail Malcolm Hail King of Scotland Hail.

NOTE:

I have to express my profound gratitude to Quinn Harris (director) and Jack Paterson (production dramaturg) who invited me to attend rehearsals for the staging of the English translation, commissioned and co-produced by Theatre Conspiracy and GasHeart Theatre, which premiered May 20, 2011, in Vancouver, BC, Canada. Our collaboration provided the opportunity of refining the text with the actors for its final version.

ANATOMY TITUS FALL OF ROME

A Shakespeare Commentary

Translated by Carl Weber and Paul David Young

Humanity's
Veins opened like a book
Pages turning in the stream of blood

CHARACTERS

SATURNINUS

BASSIANUS

TITUS ANDRONICUS

MARCUS ANDRONICUS

LUCIUS

QUINTUS

MARTIUS

MUTIUS

AARON, THE MOOR

TAMORA

CHIRON

DEMETRIUS

LAVINIA

PUBLIUS

AEMILIUS

VALENTINE

CAIUS

CLOWN

MESSENGER

NURSE

BOY

GOTHS, TRIBUNES, ATTENDANTS OF SATURNINUS

1

A NEW VICTORY WASTES ROME THE CAPITAL
OF THE WORLD TWO SONS OF A DEAD EMPEROR
EACH SON FOLLOWED BY HIS GANG OF THUGS
HAS MADE HIS CLAIM TO THE EMPTY THRONE
ONE SON WITH THE RIGHT OF THE FIRST-BORN
THE OTHER SON BRAGS ABOUT HIS MERITS
BETWEEN THEM THE IMPERIAL CROWN IN HIS WEAK HAND
STANDS THE OLDEST TRIBUNE BROTHER OF
COMMANDER TITUS ADRONICUS WHO
FOR TEN YEARS HAS WAGED WAR AGAINST THE GOTHS
WHO OUT OF THE FORESTS AND STEPPES
SWARM AGAINST THE TROUGHS OF CITIES ALREADY
DECIMATED BY WOLVES BAD HARVESTS STORMS
THE MESSENGER WHO REPORTED VICTORY
LIES WITH HIS LUNGS RIPPED OPEN ON THE STAIRS
TO THE CAPITOL THE CANDIDATES WAVE
THEIR SWORDS AND INCITE THEIR FOLLOWERS
TO END THE POWER STRUGGLE BEFORE
THE PEOPLE ENTHRONE THE VICTOR OF FIVE WARS
TITUS ANDRONICUS FIRST SWORD OF ROME
POSSESSED OF EVERY VIRTUE ROME REQUIRES
I Saturninus I am Caesar
I Bassianus I am Caesar
MARCHING BOOTS SHAKE THE METAL WALLS OF SLUMS
OUTSIDE THE CITY AND ON THE TOWERS
GUARDS SEE DUSTY COLUMNS RAISED BY MARCHING
ROME WAITS FOR THE BOOTY NEW SLAVES FOR
THE LABOR MARKET FOR THE BROTHELS FRESH FLESH
GOLD FOR THE BANKS WEAPONS FOR THE ARMORY

THE PEOPLE WHO WAIT IN SAUSAGE STALLS AND
BEER TENTS CHEER THEIR LIVING AND DEAD HEROES
AND IN THE EMPTY SOCCER STADIUMS
ROLLING DICE AND BUZZED BY SWARMS OF FLIES
SOMETIMES SOMEONE KILLS TWO OR THREE OF THEM
WITH AXE AND FASCES THE LICTORS WAIT FOR
REPLACEMENTS FOR THE UNDERWORLD'S BASEMENT
HAILED BY CHOIRS OF CHILDREN THE PARADE
COFFINS IN FRONT INSIDE THEM DEAD SONS
INVITE THE YOUTH TO CHASE AFTER THE DEAD
INTO DEATH AND INTO GLORY FOUR SONS
ARE STILL LIVING STILL FOUR STANDARD-BEARERS
THEY NUMBERED TWENTY AFTER THE FIRST VICTORY
THE DEAD PLEBIANS ROT IN MASS GRAVES
THE GIRLS UNBUTTON THEIR BLOUSES AND TOSS
FLOWERS IN FRONT OF THE TREADS OF TANKS
GREAT ROME THE WHORE OF CORPORATIONS TAKES
UP HER WOLVES TO SUCK HER BREASTS AGAIN
CRAWLING IN THE DUST OF THE VICTORS
THE VANQUISHED THE GOTHS THIS TIME A QUEEN
WITH HEAVY BREASTS HER NEGRO ON A CHAIN
THE BLACK ONE AND THE PRINCES BEHIND HER
STILL THERE ARE THREE THE VICTORS PLAY MUSIC
AND CRAM THE DEAD INTO THE FAMILY TOMB
MOURNING DEMANDS REVENGE BLOOD GUZZLES BLOOD
THE FIRST-BORN ADMONISHES THE COMMANDER
The dead don't like to be alone Sacrifice
The queen of the Goths has three sons left
That's one too many Give us her first-born
THE QUEEN OF THE GOTHS FALLS TO HER KNEES
BEFORE THE SWORDS HER BREASTS SWEEPING THE DUST
BUT OF COURSE WHATEVER HAPPENS HAPPENS

You men of Rome oh great Andronicus
Victorious commander See my tears
Shed for my son Look at these breasts They gave
Him the milk that formed his character
Do you want to slaughter him in the streets
Of Rome because he was a tiger for
His fatherland like your sons were for Rome
If you want to act like the gods have mercy
Sorry madam he dies We have a custom
To reconcile with the shadows of our dead
Those down under scream
Rome do you hear my scream
NOT YOURS MADAM SAYS THE COMMANDER AND
WORDLESSLY TO MAKE FOOD FOR THEIR BROTHERS'
JOURNEY INTO THE VOID THE SONS SLAUGHTER
THE GOTHIC PRINCE WHO SCREAMS FOR HIS MOTHER
THE FIRST-BORN WHO WAS NEXT IN LINE TO RULE
IF SHE STILL RULED SHE WHO KISSES THE DUST
THEY BUTCHER HIS LIMBS SO THAT THE HEROES
CAN WALK ON THE PATH OF HIS BLOOD MORE LIGHTLY
INTO THE VOID THE SISTER WATCHES
NOT THE FIRST TIME LICKS NOT THE FIRST TIME
THE BLOOD OF ENEMIES OFF THE HAND
OF THE VICTOR HER COMMANDER FATHER
Peace and honor to my father Titus
To my dead brothers my guilty tears
And my love to my bridegroom Bassianus
The second son of Caesar and his heir
MUTELY THE GOTH QUEEN SCREAMS HER MOTHER'S CRY
THE REST BELONGS TO CAESAR WHO IS CAESAR
I Saturninus I am Caesar
I Bassianus I am Caesar

Heiner Müller After Shakespeare

AND ONE VOICE BECOMES A WHISPERING CHORUS
WHICH RINGS IN THE EARS OF THE CANDIDATES
Titus should be Caesar THE COMMANDER'S THANKS
HIS TEMPLES TOO GRAY HIS COURAGE TOO TIRED
THE SWORD TOO HEAVY FOR HIS OLD ARM
BECAUSE OF THE WEIGHT OF BLOOD TURNED TO METAL
HE RIPS THE CROWN FROM HIS BROTHER'S WEAKER
HAND AND THROWS IT TO THE FIRST-BORN SON
A good steep pass-off THE NERVOUS SWEATY
HAND OF THE CHOSEN ONE DROPS THE HEIRLOOM
HE CRAWLS TO IT TO FISH IT FROM THE MUD
SWEATY-HANDED SATURNINUS CAESAR IN ROME
TO WHOM THE COMMANDER GIVES HIS DAUGHTER
SO HE WILL BE CONNECTED THROUGH HER WOMB
JUST AS BY HIS SWORD HE IS BOUND TO HIM
ADMITTEDLY SHE'S ALREADY ENGAGED
BUT ROME IS ROME AND CAESAR IS CAESAR
THE PEOPLE CHEER HIS CHOICE LOUDLY THEY NEED
NOT CHEER SO MUCH AMID SO MUCH MOURNING
A CROWN WILL FIT ON ANY PERSON'S HEAD
THE NEW CAESAR REACHES FOR HIS PRESENT
HIS BROTHER'S BRIDE FROM THE COMMANDER'S HAND
THE CHORUS OF SONS SINGS FOR THE SCORNED ONE
THE OTHER CANDIDATE WHO CLAIMS THE THRONE
THEN THEY WAVE THEIR SWORDS She is his bride
Our sister She was promised to him
THE COMMANDER IS CAESAR'S COMMANDER
IN HIS HAND THE SWORD BECOMES LIGHT FOR ROME
IT KILLS ONE SON HOWEVER IT'S NOT LIGHT
ENOUGH TO KILL ALL HIS REMAINING SONS
THE BRIDE OF CAESAR FALLS TO THE BRIDEGROOM
THE COMMANDER'S SONS COVER HIS RETREAT

THE COMMANDER CRIES Treason AND YELLS FOR GUARDS
CAESAR HAD SEEN TO THAT AND IN PLAIN VIEW
THE RIPE BREASTS OF THE CONQUERED GOTHIC QUEEN
HE DRAGS THIS FLESHY PRIZE INTO THE PALACE
THE NEGRO SHARPENS HIS TEETH ON THE CHAIN
THE COMMANDER IS DIVIDED BY HIS SWORD
HALF ROMAN HALF FATHER OF HIS CHILDREN
BETWEEN THE LAUGHTER AND THE CROWD'S APPLAUSE
RIPS OPEN HIS BREAST FOR THE TV SCREENS
AND SHOWS THE TRIBUNES HIS BEATING HEART
HIS VOICE BREAKS CALLING IN THE EMPTINESS
You traitors Give the emperor his bride
THE EMPEROR'S ANSWER FROM HIS COMMAND TOWER
HIS HAND GROPING THE GOTH QUEEN'S PUBIC HAIR
No Titus no Caesar doesn't need her
Nor you Nor anyone from your stable
I trust no one who has ever mocked me
Not you nor any of your treacherous
Sons who are allied to dishonor me
Was there no one in Rome as good a clown
As Saturninus Very well Andronicus
Your cheating matches your boasting that I
Took power from your hand like a beggar
Go on your way Pay out your loose change to
The one who waves around his sword for her
A valiant son-in-law a brilliant choice
Who will doubtlessly bring you so much joy
Gifted with your sons who have grown so wild
At play in the Commonwealth of Rome
Tamora Empress come with me my nymph.
ROME'S COMMANDER CLOSES HIS HANDS ON HIS SWORD
THESE WORDS CUT LIKE A KNIFE RIGHT THROUGH MY HEART

WHAT CAESAR HAD A WEDDING WITHOUT TITUS
TITUS WHEN DID YOU WALK ALONE IN ROME
IN SUCH SHAME AND SO UNJUSTLY ACCUSED
HOME FROM BRIDE-ROBBING TO MURDEROUS FATHER
TO BURY THE DEAD BROTHER AND NEPHEW
THE ROBBERS WAIL THE MURDERER IS STONE
THE PEOPLE ROAR A FOLK SONG FROM THE BEER TENT
ACCOMPANIED BY THE MILITARY BRASS BAND
THE SONG OF THE DEAD BROTHER NEPHEW SON
KILLED FOR ROME BY ROME'S FAITHFUL COMMANDER
TO HONOR ROME AND NOW SCORNED BY ROME
THE ANDRONICI FAMILY WAR RAGES
Oh Titus look oh look what you have done
In an angry fight you slayed your son.
False tribune No not a son you didn't
Nor these accomplices of such a deed
Which stains our shield these relatives
Unworthy brothers quite unworthy sons.
But let's bury him as is our custom.
Away traitor in this grave he won't rest
Five hundred years this monument has stood
Which I lately peopled and with glory
Only soldiers and servants of Rome sleep here
In glory No one killed in petty fights.
Bury him where you can no place for him here.
He will be buried beside his brothers
He will be or we'll join him in the grave.
He will be What's his name the rogue who said that.
BROTHER AND SONS ARE CRAWLING ON THEIR KNEES
BEFORE THE BROTHER WHO STABBED THE NEPHEW
BEFORE THE FATHER WHO STABBED THE BROTHER
FOR THEIR PLACE IN THE FAMILY HARBOR

THE MURDERER SPITS TWO TEARS ON THE DEAD
To be dishonored in Rome by my sons.
All right dig his ditch And dump me in too.
A NEW PICTURE IN THE FAMILY ALBUM
A NEW COFFIN STUFFED IN THE FAMILY TOMB
THE REST IS POLITICS RIGHT ON CUE TWO
GATES SPRING OPEN AND VOMIT TWO COUPLES
FOR A DOUBLE WEDDING NUMBER ONE IS
CAESAR THE CROWN ASKEW ON HIS SWEATY
BALD HEAD HE IS RIDDEN BY HIS GOTH QUEEN
WHO UNBRIDLED BRIDLES HER NEGRO IN
ROMAN LIVERY MUSCLES DRAWN TAUGHT AGAINST
THE UNFAMILIAR FABRIC THE CREASES
THREATEN REVENGE NEW DEATH AND ANARCHY
THE SONS IMPUDENT IN ROMAN COSTUME
STUTTER LATIN THEIR TONGUES HEAVY WITH WINE
OF THE ENEMY NUMBER TWO THE BROTHER
WITH HIS VIRGIN SPIFFIED UP FOR THE WEDDING
LIKE SNOW HER BREASTS GLIMMERING THROUGH HER GOWN
THE POINTS PLANT SPEARS IN THE EYES OF THE GOTH
PRINCES WHOSE LOOKS SNOW BLOOD TO SPICE UP
THE PARTY A LITTLE POISON IS SPRAYED
THE EMPEROR IS THE FIRST TO SPEAK
So Bassianus this round went to you
May God give you joy Sir with your new bride.
And you with yours my Lord I say no more
And I wish you no less than all the best.
Traitor
If Rome has laws and we have power
You should regret this theft you and your gang.
I took what is mine and you call it theft.
It's fine Sir You are short with us and if

85

We want to live we will be sharp with you.
I will expect it But your duty to
Rome is to take back into your favor
This noble man Lord Titus wounded in
His reputation and his honor who
To preserve the daughter for you alone
Killed his youngest son with his own hand he
Who was a father to you and a friend
To Rome in all his deeds.
Prince Bassianus
Don't you dare commend my deeds you who stole
My honor in league with these The heavens
And Rome are my witnesses that I did
Always love and honor Saturninus.
My dearest Lord If ever Tamora
Was pretty in your imperial eye
Forgive what's past Sweety do it for me.
How Madam is publicly disgraced and
Like a slave departs quite without vengeance.
CAESAR WOULD LIKE TO CALL THE LICTORS BUT
THE GOTH QUEEN KISSES THE COMMAND FROM HIS LIPS.
You are too freshly planted on your throne
The people and the tribunes are behind him
Show mercy now The rest is my business
AND WHISPERS IN THE LANGUAGE OF HER HEART
I'll find a day to slaughter all of them
And uproot their entire race the bloodhound of
The father and the traitors all his sons
With whom I pleaded to save my son's life
On my school bench they will learn their lesson
They'll kneel in the streets and cry for mercy
And get as much mercy in the streets of Rome

As their knees will get from the paving stones
THE EMPRESS HAS A SMILE FOR THE COMMANDER
Come sweet emperor come Andronicus
Lift up the good old man and warm his heart
Which curdles in the storm from your eyebrows.
Titus stand up It's what the empress wants.
Others should find forgiveness on their knees.
THE COMMANDER FORCES HIS SONS TO THEIR KNEES
AND LICKS THE HAND OF THE GOTH QUEEN ONLY
YESTERDAY CONQUERED BY HIM EMPRESS NOW
IN ROME AND THE SUN THAT WARMS OR BURNS HIM
THE GOTH QUEEN HAS BIGGER PLANS FOR HIM AND
ROME THAN A QUICK INSULT WHICH STINGS JUST ONCE
BEHIND THE VEIL OF HER KIND SMILE THERE SLEEPS
IN THE ABYSS OF HER EYES A DREAM OF
A LONG AND WIDE-RANGING RETALIATION
CROOKED IN THE BOWELS OF THE HATED ONES
THE COMMANDER INVITES CAESAR TO HUNT
ON THE MORNING AFTER THE WEDDING NIGHT
WITH HORN AND HOUND AGAINST THE FOREST BEASTS
A BIT OF BLOODSHED IN GOOD COMPANY
THEN THE WEDDING MARCH CAUSES HEARTS TO MELT
IN THE PALACE YARD THE PEOPLE DANCE
THE NEGRO HAS NO HEART HE'S FREEZING IN ROME
NOT HIS WEDDING THAT BOOMS FROM THE PALACE
DOG AND BITCH ENTANGLED NEXT TO HIM
FORNICATING IN THE VACANT SQUARE HOWLING
IN THEIR SAD ATTEMPT TO SEPARATE WHAT
INSTINCT UNITED A MONSTER WITH TWO
HEADS EACH WANTS TO TEAR ITSELF FREE STEAMING
WITH SWEAT AND LONELY IN THEIR MISERY
UNTIL THE NEGRO KICKS THEM LOOSE HE NEEDS

THE PLAZA TO PERFORM HIS MONOLOG
Oh Tamora oh flower of my life you
Empress in Rome capital of the world
Stomp on your heart and collect your wits Moor
When you climb to the top after your whore
Virtue crawls on its knees before her blink
The eagles of Rome wriggle in her net
The Negro is riding an empress
Pearls and gold wait for me to snatch them up
My black hide will glisten with riches
Caesar reins the horse the Negro rides it
Count your days Rome Who's ranting here
Two Gothic louts.
Your years have lost their
Wit Chiron Your wit is dull and pointless
And rudely forces itself onto my place.
Your year or is it two of advantage
Makes me no less horny nor stiffens your luck
I am as ready and able as you
To service the lady with distinction
I will demonstrate with my iron thing
That I know the way to Lavinia's heart.
Do you also know where a lady's heart beats.
Draw and your name is what's left of your manhood.
Get a bludgeon two lovers run over.
THE NEGRO GRABS THE GOTH BOYS BY THE NECK
LIKE DOLLS AND THEY FUMBLE WITH THEIR SWORDS
AGAINST EACH OTHER FIRMLY IN HIS GRIP
Tell me little boy whose silly mother
Tied a sharp toy around his waist how do
You have the nerve to piss a real man off
Let your thing stay glued in its scabbard

Until you have learned how to use it.
Permit me sir with my small gifts to let
You have a clear feeling for who I am.
Hey boy are you getting cheeky.
Stop stop gentlemen.
Not before my iron sticks in his breast
And his mouth is cram-full of his own blood.
Just try it and impale yourself on my
Iron coward whose tongue thunders because
He cannot get it up with his weapon.
Are you crazy You will die for an itch
That any old bump in the night can scratch.
I will die a thousand deaths Negro
If Lavinia but once belongs to me.
You are in Rome In Rome it's the custom
That the bride belongs to the bridegroom.
Not this one
Boy pick something you have a chance to get
Lavinia is the hope of your brother.
What Do you want to sheathe your swords in the
Scabbards of each others' bleeding bodies
Or mount Lavinia's bed and there do
Your thrusting the one with the other.
Demetrius before Chiron.
Chiron before
Demetrius.
If you die after me Draw.
Stay your weapons and be reasonable
What divides you unites you Are you Christians
That you know only one way Why not
All at once and from several angles.
Your advice dude shows us your valiant taste.

Now Negro create the opportunity.
Do not hope for her love She belongs to
Bassianus brother of Caesar whom we love
We must do it Your mother is his wife
Pleasure is free when force knows the way
I know the way my Lords A hunt is afoot
The Roman ladies will be on parade
The paths through the forest twist and wind
Nature has room for all kinds of crime
Lure your doe away from the herd there
Don't whisper sweet nothings take her by force
You can count on me as well as the empress
Who is aware of your new appetites
She's an expert in the art of vengeance
She's filled the bridegroom so full of wine that
He hardly knows himself much less his bride
Who makes your trousers bulge You have the jump
The court of Caesar boils over with gossip
The palace is full of tongues eyes ears
The forest has no mercy deaf black dumb
There you heroes relieve yourselves of pain
Unseen by the heavens have your pleasure
And together take your flame's measure
THE GOTH BOYS EMPTY THEIR POCKETS TWO LUMPS
OF GOLD FROM THEIR FIRST HASTY PINCHES
OUT OF AN IMPERIAL TREASURE CHEST
SOME TIP MONEY FOR THE NEGRO WHO STUFFS
IT GOLD ON GOLD IN HIS LOINCLOTH WHERE HIS
BEAUTIFUL MEMBER RESTS AND WAITS THERE FOR
CAESAR TO SLEEP NIGHT BLACKENS ROME THE NIGHT
OF THE NEGRO HIS SEX DREAMS OF AFRICA
HIS SEMEN A LIGHTNING TRACE WHITE IN BLACK

THE LIGHTNING CHANGES ROME INTO A FOREST
PEOPLED WITH BEASTS OF HIS NATIVE LAND
THERE HE WAITS FOR HIS OTHER HUNT BUT WITH
A CHANGE OF ROLES THE HUNTER IS THE PREY
WITH TOOTH AND CLAW INSTEAD OF HORN AND HOUND

DIGRESSION ABOUT THE SLEEP OF THE METROPOLIS

GRASS BLASTS THE STONE THE WALLS GROW FLOWERS
THE FOUNDATIONS SWEAT THE BLOOD OF SLAVES
THE BREATH OF WILDCATS WAFTS THROUGH PARLIAMENT
WITH ITS HOT CLOUD THE STENCH OF CARRION
HYENA SHADOWS SWEEP AND VULTURES FLY
THROUGH AVENUES AND STAIN TRIUMPHAL COLUMNS
THE PANTHERS LEAP WITHOUT A SOUND THROUGH THE
    BANKS
ALL BECOMES A SHORE AND WAITS FOR THE SEA
DOWN IN THE SLUDGE OF THE SEWER SYSTEM
HANNIBAL'S DEAD ELEPHANTS ARE TRUMPETING
THE SCOUTS OF ATTILA WALK DRESSED AS TOURISTS
THROUGH THE MUSEUMS AND THEY BITE THE MARBLE
THEY MEASURE THE CHURCHES FOR THEIR HORSES'
STABLES AND ROAM GREEDY THROUGH THE SUPERMARKET
WITHIN A YEAR THEIR HORSES' HOOVES
WILL STOMP AND KISS THE COLONIAL LOOT
BRINGING THE FIRST WORLD HOME TO NOTHINGNESS

2

Titus, Marcus, Quintus, Marius and others.
TITUS   The hunt is on, and grey the morning light
The fields are steaming and green stands the forest.
Unchain the hounds and may their barking wake
The emperor and his Gothic bride
The prince too. And may the hunting horn speak
That the palace trembles with its echo.
Sons, make it your duty as it is ours,
To pay attention to Ceasar's person.
I had a worrisome sleep today and
The new day has done little to cheer me.
Saturninus, Tamora, Bassianus, Lavinia.
Many good mornings to your majesty.
And to you madam as many and as good.
That was the hunter's greeting as promised.
SATURNINUS   And you have blown well, barked well though somewhat
On the early side for newlywed brides
BASSIANUS   Lavinia, what do you say.
LAVINIA   I say no.
I've been wide awake for two hours or more.
SATURNINUS   Lady, now you shall see
The Roman hunt.
MARCUS   I have such hounds, my Lord
That can chase down the proudest of panthers
They'll clamber to the crest of the mountains.
TITUS   And I have horses that follow the hunt
As fast as swallows, barely touching the ground.
Chiron, Demetrius.
DEMETRIUS   Brother, we hunt with neither horse nor hound
But we know a certain doe will soon be found.

3

Aaron.

THE NEGRO IS HIS OWN DIRECTOR
HE DRAWS THE CURTAIN WRITES THE PLOT PROMPTS
TEACHES HIS WOLVES TO EXERCISE THEIR FANGS
ON THE DOE OF THE DAY KILL A STAG THEY
LEARN QUICKLY ON THEIR FIRST DAY AT SCHOOL
HE SHOVELS IN THE PIT WHAT CROSSES HIM
AND WITH HIS MARKED CARDS HE PLAYS HIS GAME
IN THE THEATRE OF HIS BLACK REVENGE

AARON   Whoever's got brains might think I've got none
To bury this nice gold under a tree
Without any intent to see it again.
Whoever looks down on me should know that
This gold is minted for a plan that
Cleverly promoted will hatch from me
A piece of villainy not found in any book.
Sleep, my sweet gold, and wait for your hour
You're the price on the heads of three Roman dogs.
The deal, I hope, will flush out from his rest
The frog that helps himself to my treasure chest.
Tamora.
TAMORA   My dear Aaron, why do you look so sadly
At nature which paints its face with joy
The birds are singing from every shrub
The snake curls up in the gaze of the sun
The leaves shake verdantly in the cool wind
And throw shadow patterns on the moss.
In its sweet twilight, Aaron, as echo

Apes the hounds with blabla and their yelping
To the hunting horn's melody as loud
As if there were double the hunt afoot
We will place ourselves far from their noise
And after the duel which, one supposes
The wandering prince and Dido conducted
As a fortunate storm surprised them
And behind the curtain of a mute cave
We will, entangled in each others' arms
Crown our desire with a golden sleep.
And horn and hound and melody of the birds
Will be our singsong of the nanny
The hushabye that lulls the brood to sleep.
AARON   If Venus guides your wishing, madam
Saturn is the ruler of my desire.
This my eye shows, which keeps death in sight
My silence and cloudy melancholy
My woolen fleece that's ruffling its curls
Like a snake when it uncoils itself
To carry out a fatal judgment.
Those are not the signs of Venus, madam
My heart beats revenge, death shelters in my hand
Blood and justice go around in my brain.
Listen, Tamora, empress of my soul
Which wants no greater heaven than your body
Today's the Lord's Day for our friend Bassianus
His Philomele will lose her tongueAnd your sons will rob her of her chastity
And wash hand in hand in Bassianus's blood.
Do you see this letter here, take it, I say
And give unto Caesar this scrap of fate.
It is the plot of our tragedy
The central theme is our enemies' blood.

Don't ask more. Someone's looking at us
Here comes one part of our future prey
Clueless about what's flowering in his life.
Bassianus, Lavinia.
TAMORA   Ah my sweet Moor, sweeter than my own life.
AARON   Quiet, great empress, here comes Bassianus.
Pick a fight with him and I'll get your sons
To soothe your quarrel with their assistance.
Aaron exits.
BASSIANUS   What do we see here. Rome's high empress
Denuded of her retinue of decency
Or is it Diana, costumed as such
And having forsaken her holy grove
To observe the hunt in the forest.
TAMORA   Impudent spy, who dogs my every step.
Had I the power ascribed to Diana
Right now I would implant on your temples
The horns of Acteon and my hounds would
Fight each other to get at this fresh prey
Which the hunt has made of the hunter.
LAVINIA   If you'll permit me to speak, high empress
It's said, you have a gift for planting horns.
Could it be that you have dared to unite
Yourself with your Negro in such an effort.
May Zeus protect your lordship from his dogs.
Crying shame if they mistook him for a stag.
BASSIANUS   Believe me, queen, your black antipode
Makes your honor look like his skin stained
Disgusting and wholly detestable.
Why would you go about apart from your court
Dismounted from your noble snow white mare
To come here to this place of darkness

Accompanied only by a wild Negro
If not led by the reins of hot instinct.
LAVINIA   And, interrupted now in your play,
You have good reason to blacken my noble
Lord with impudence. I say, let's away
Let her frolic in her raven-colored way.
The valley is fitting for a stiff point.
BASSIANUS   Caesar, my brother, shall learn of this.
LAVINIA   Yes, he's done much learning from his mistake.
The good emperor, so sorely abused.
TAMORA   How long have I patience to endure this?
Chiron, Demitrius.
DEMETRIUS   Why is it, dear mistress, our noble mother
That your majesty looks pale and bloodless.
TAMORA   Do I have cause, do you think, to be pale.
These two here have lured me to this place
An ugly desert valley, you can see
With trees that summer doesn't dress in leaves
Overgrown with moss and mistletoe run wild
The sun does not shine here nothing breeds
Only night owls and deadly the raven.
They showed me the fearful gorge and said
That in the dead hours of the night there wander
Thousands of ghosts, thousands of snakes hiss
Ten thousand toads spew poison, hedgehogs stare
With such bewildered terrible screams
That just to hear it all mortal flesh falls
Into madness or dies right on the spot.
They had hardly dished up this hellish tale
Than they promised that they were going to tie
Me to the stump of this deformed yew-tree
And leave me to a miserable death

And scolded me as an adulteress
And Gothic goat and more bitter names
Of vile abuse than any ear has heard.
And if you had not wondrously appeared
They'd have executed their deed on me.
If you love your mother, revenge her life
Or I disown you as my children.
Demetrius and Chiron kill Bassianus.
LAVINIA   Ah, Semiramis, barbarian, Tamora
One can only call you by your name.
TAMORA   Give me the knife, my sons, and see how
Your mother's hand clears your mother's name.
DEMETRIUS   Stop, Mother, she's entitled to more than that.
First thresh the wheat, and then burn the straw.
The dolly put on fine airs over her
Chastity, wedding vows, fidelity
And blackened your majesty with such ink.
Should she carry this burden to her grave.
CHIRON   And if she does, I'll be a eunuch first.
We'll stuff the husband into his secret hole
Make his carcass a pillow for our pleasure.
TAMORA   And once you have the honey that we like
Be sure the wasp doesn't live to sting us.
CHIRON   I swear to you, madam, we'll play it safe.
Madam, let's violently celebrate
The preservation of your marriage.
LAVINIA   Oh Tamora, you wear a woman's face –
TAMORA   Does she speak. I won't hear it. Away with her.
LAVANIA   Dear lords, make her hear me, only one word.
DEMETRIUS   Listen, pretty lady, let it be your fame
To see her tears. Let your heart be without
Any mercy, like a stone to raindrops.

97

LAVINIA   Has the tiger's brood ever taught the tigress.
Oh don't make her rage, you have her tooth
The milk you drank from her turned to marble
You sucked tyranny from her very tits
Not every mother could breed such sons.
Please ask her for a woman's pity.
CHIRON   What. You want me to become a bastard.
LAVINIA   It's true, the raven doesn't hatch a lark.
But I've heard, if I could only think of it now:
The lion, moved by pity, they say
Gave way and let his kingly claws be clipped.
People say, ravens raise lost children
They will let their own brood starve in the nest.
Even if your hard heart says no, give me
If not much goodness, a little pity.
TAMORA   I don't know what that is, away with her.
LAVINIA   Let me teach you something. For my father's
Sake who gave you life, instead of killing you
Don't be stubborn, open up your deaf ears.
TAMORA   If you hadn't insulted me in person
It's because of him I have no pity.
My sons, do you remember the tears
I shed to save your brother from slaughter
But he stood there unmoved, Andronicus.
Therefore, take her and use her as you please
The worse you do, the better I'll love it.
LAVINIA   Oh Tamora, be a queen and noble
And kill me here with your very own hands.
Life isn't the reason that I pleaded
To save Bassianus when he died I was killed.
TAMORA   Why are you begging, woman. Let me go.
LAVINIA   I ask for a quick death and one thing more

Which my tongue cannot bring itself to say.
Save me from their lust, it's worse than murder
Throw me into some nauseating grave
Where the eyes of men will never see me
Be merciful and be my murderer.
TAMORA   Steal from my own sons. I won't
They'll have you for their sport see if they don't.
DEMETRIUS   Away with her. You held us up too long.
LAVINIA   Not a shred of mercy. You're no woman
You beast, you defame the name of woman.
If I were a man —
CHIRON   I'll shut her trap. You bring me the husband.
Here is his hole, which Aaron chose for him.
TAMORA   Sons, fare well. See to it, you proceed safely.
My heart will never sound a happy beat
Until all the Andronici are dead.
I'll go to my sweet Moor to pass an hour.
For my Goths, this Roman woman to deflower.
Lavinia, Chiron, Demetrius, Tamora exit. Aaron, Quintus, Martius.
AARON   Come along, my Lords, hurry, shake a leg.
Very soon I'll show you the stinking pit
Where I saw the panther deep asleep.
QUINTUS   My vision is blurry, how can that be.
MARTIUS   Brother, if it weren't a question of honor
I'd gladly quit the hunt and sleep a little.
QUINTUS   Did you fall. What ingenious pit
The mouth covered with a wild growth of bushes
From whose leaves there drips freshly shed blood
As fresh as morning dew, the sweat of flowers.
This place signals death, so it seems to me.
Brother, did you hurt yourself when you fell.
MARTIUS   Yes, brother, injured by the worst picture

Ever seen by eyes, ever dug into a heart.

AARON   I'll go get Caesar, so he'll find them

May the discovery help him divine

How the two of them butchered his brother.

Aaron exits.

MARTIUS   Brother, why aren't you helping me get up

Out of this terrible blood-splattered pit.

QUINTUS   I am seized by an unfamiliar fear

A cold sweat sets my limbs to trembling

My heart fears even more than my eyes can see.

MARTIUS   To test whether your heart suspects the truth

Aaron and you, have a look inside here

And see this black picture of blood and death.

QUINTUS   Aaron is gone, and my pitiful heart

Refuses to permit my eyes to see

That thing before which foreboding trembles.

Oh tell me who that is, because I was

Never a child scared of what I don't know.

MARTIUS   Bassianus lies here, radiant in his blood

A bundle of death, slaughtered like a lamb.

QUINTUS   In the darkness how do you know it's he.

MARTIUS   Because he wears on his bloody finger

A precious ring that illuminates the pit

And like a candle in a crypt shines

On the earth-toned cheeks of the dead man

And discovers the bowels of his grave.

Like the pale moon that shone on Pyramus

Where he lay at night, bathed in maiden blood.

Oh brother, if fear has weakened you

As it has me, help me with your weak hand

Out of this awful pit greedy for blood

Full of dread like the foggy mouth of hell.

QUINTUS   Give me your hand so I can help you out.
If I lack the strength for so much help
The hungry womb will swallow me up too
The poor grave of poor Prince Bassianus.
I haven't the strength to lift you to the edge.
MARTIUS   And I'm too weak to climb up without help.
QUINTUS   Give me your hand again, I won't let go
Until you're up here or I'm down there.
If you can't come to me, I'll come to you.
Saturninus, Aaron.
SATURNINUS   I want to see this pit with my own eyes
And who it was who jumped in just now.
Say who you are, you who just climbed down
In this pit which gapes open in the earth.
MARTIUS   The unfortunate sons of old Titus
Who were brought here in an unhappy hour
To find Bassianus, your brother, dead.
SATURNINUS   My brother is dead. You must be joking.
They are at the hunting lodge, he and his bride
On the north end of this happy preserve.
I saw them alive not an hour ago.
MARTIUS   We don't know where you saw them living still
But here, oh misery, we found him dead.
TAMORA   Where is my lord Caesar.
SATURNINUS   Here, Tamora, in the stranglehold of grief.
TAMORA   Where is Bassianus, your brother.
SATURNINUS   You touch the very depth of my wound
That poor man, Bassianus, lies here murdered.
TAMORA   Then I've come too late with this deadly writ
The plan for this untimely tragedy.
I am astonished at how the human
Face can mask bloody ambition in smiles.

SATURNINUS *reads:*
"And if we're fortunate enough to meet him
Bassianus is who we mean, dear hunter
Then you're the one to dig his grave for him
You know what we mean. Look for your reward
In the nettles of the elderberry
Shadowing the opening of the pit
In which by our will he'll be laid to rest
Do it and forever call us your friends."
Oh Tamora, who ever heard of such.
This is the pit, here the elderberry.
See, my lords, if you can find the hunter
Who was supposed to bury Bassianus here.
AARON   My gracious lord, here is the sack of gold.
SATURNINUS   Two of your pups, curs from the bloody race
Who have robbed my brother of his life.
Sirs, drag them from this pit into prison.
There they'll wait until I think of some kind
Of torture that no one has imagined.
TAMORA   Are they in the pit. This wonder shows how
Short the distance is from murder to death.
TITUS   Your majesty, Caesar, on my weak knee
With tears from one who finds it hard to cry
That this guilt should rest with my cursed sons
Cursed if this guilt were to be proved –
SATURNINUS   It will be proved. A blind man could see it.
Who found the letter. Tamora, was it you.
TAMORA   Andronicus himself discovered it.
TITUS   That I did, my lord. Let me vouch for them.
I swear on my father's honorable grave
At your royal wish they shall stand ready
To answer these accusations with their lives.

SATURNINUS   You're no bail bondsman. Look you, follow me.
Take the dead body and his murderers.
Not one word more from those two, their guilt is clear.
One thing I know: if there were a worse end
Than death it should be executed on them.
TAMORA   Andronicus, I will plead with Caesar
For your sons to have a happy end.
TITUS   Come, Lucius, we won't say another word.

4

FROM THE WOODS IT SPRAYS WITH BLOOD SPRINGS THE ROE
OF DAY COMMENTED UPON BY ITS HUNTERS
A WORK OF ART THROUGH VIOLENCE A TRIUMPH
OF LOGIC WORD AND WRITING ARE DETACHED
THEIR WORK DONE THE ARTISTS GO ON THEIR WAY
HOPING THAT THEIR FAME WILL NEVER REACH THEM
THE EXHIBITED WORK OF ART RUNS BACK AND
FORTH ON THE CATWALK OF THE THEATRE
BETWEEN HUMAN AND HUMAN IN THE OCEAN
OF FEAR THE FEAR OF THE AUDIENCE NO HUMAN
IS ON THE STAGE MACHINES TALK PLAY GO FEAR
THE PLAYER SITS BELOW NOT A HUMAN
MACHINES LAUGH AND WHISPER RUSTLE THEIR CLOTHES
AND NOW AND THEN THEY CLAP WITH THEIR HANDS
GLASS EYE STARES LIGHT UP OUT OF THE DARKNESS
THE POET SINGS HIS SONG KEEPS ITS HUMOR
HUMOR OF THE BUTCHER OR OF DESPAIR
THE PRODUCT OF THE GOTHIC ART OF LOVE
THE BLOOD IN HIS MOUTH DOESN'T CHOKE HIS VOICE
IT SOARS UP TO HAUNTINGLY EERIE HEIGHTS
SHAMELESS HE SECURES ON HIS FACE THE MASK

OF THE HORNY UNCLE WHO KNOWS MANY
ARTS AND HIS MASK GROWS ONTO MY SKIN WHY
DOESN'T HIS VOICE BREAK WHY DOESN'T MINE BREAK
WHICH SINGS ALONG WITH HIM HIS BLOOD-SOAKED TEXT
IN THE MISERABLE GHETTOS OF HIS SOUL
IN MY DREAMS THEY ARE MY LODGING THERE WAITS
A MURDERER NOT SPEAKING BIDES HIS TIME
WHO SOMETIMES KNOCKS ON THE THIN CEILING
AS IF HE WISHED TO TEASE THE INHABITANTS
Here I am Here I am And now I'm not.
WHEN THEY STAND WITH THEIR CUDGELS IN ONE DOOR
HE'S KNOCKING FROM ONE OF THE OTHER ROOMS
Here I am Yes it's me the mocking killer
Do you hear my knife buzz See you soon my dears
AS IN THE MARCUS PLAZA THE CAT WHO
LEARNED FROM THE DOG HOW TO SWEEP WITH ITS TAIL
IT SWEEPS ON THE GROUND AN INVISIBLE DUST
BUT IF A TOURIST WERE TO PET ITS COAT
WITHDRAWN NAILS ARE READY TO CLAW OPEN
THE VEINS OF THE PATRON IN THE ERA
OF TOURISM MURDER IS A MERCY
TO LOOK MEANS THE SAME AS KILL THE PICTURES
IN THE GREY COAT OF MY NOBODY'S NAME
YOUR MURDERER WILLIAM SHAKESPEARE IS MY
MURDERER HIS MURDER IS MY WEDDING
WILLIAM SHAKESPEARE MY NAME AND YOUR NAME GLOW
IN THE BLOOD THAT HE HAS SHED WITH OUR INK
Demetrius, Chiron, Lavinia.
DEMETRIUS   Come on, if your tongue can still speak, tell us
Who cut off your tongue and your honor.
CHIRON   Write it down what's in your head, with your hands
If your stumps know how to do your handwriting.

DEMETRIUS   Wash your tongue then, or scream with your hands.
We will leave you to your silent marching.
CHIRON   If this happened to me, I'd go hang myself.
DEMETRIUS   If you still had hands to tie the knot.
Demetrius, Chiron exit. Marcus.
MARCUS   Who is that. It is my niece on the run.
A word with you, Niece. Where is your husband.
Lavinia turns around.
Do I dream.
If only all my wealth could wake me up.
And if I am awake, then a star should
Strike me dead that I may sleep eternally.
Speak, tender niece, what untender hand
Has cut you up and denuded your body
Of its two branches, the sweet ornament
In whose shade kings have sheltered with little
Hope for half of your love. Why don't you speak
Even if your rosy lips spew forth
A crimson stream of warm blood like a
Talkative fountain that rises and falls
In the wind, comes and goes with your honeyed breath.
I see, a Tereus has plucked your flowers
And your tongue too, fearing its betrayal.
Ah, you turn away in the cloak of shame
Quite heedless of the path of the blood
A pretty spout which spits from three mouths
And with red cheeks like the face of Titan
Blushing in the embraces of a cloud.
I speak for you. Should I. I say it's so.
If I knew your heart, if I knew the beast
I could curse him and put myself at ease.
Bottled-up pain like a stopped-up oven

105

Burns the heart in which it dwells to ashes.
Beautiful Philomela lost her tongue
And still could weave a costly tapestry
About all the woes that befell her.
For you, my niece, this method is cut off.
You met a more capable Tereus
Who cut off these tender fingers that could
Weave even better than Philomela.
Had this monster seen your lily-white hands
Trembling like aspen leaves on a lute
Inviting the silken strings to kiss them
Not for his life would he have touched them so.
Had he heard the heavenly harmony
With which this tongue was gifted then he
Would have dropped his knife and fallen asleep
Like Cerberus at the Thracian singer's feet.
Shall we go and make your father blind.
A picture like you blinds a father's eye
The green field drowns in an hour-long storm
This will bring your father a year of tears.
Don't hide yourself, our hearts are all breaking
If only our howls could heal your aching.

5

THE SCENE CHANGES FROM THE FOREST OF ART
TO ROME WHERE PAPER BEATS STONE DIFFERENTLY
IN THE SANDSTORM OF LAWS ROME'S GLORIOUS
COMMANDER CRAWLS ON HIS KNEES IN FRONT OF
ROME'S BUREAUCRATS SWEEPS THE DUST WITH HIS DRESS
UNIFORM LIKE THE GOTH QUEEN DID WITH HER BREASTS
PETITIONS RUSTLE UNDERNEATH HIS KNEES

HE HAS NO EAR FOR THEM NOR THE STONE FOR HIM
ROME'S EAGLES SHIT ON THE BUTCHER OF GOTHS
UNTIL HE SHRINKS INTO HIS OWN MONUMENT
ONTO WHICH A STRAY DOG LIFTS ITS LEG
THE STONE NEEDS WATER ALL THE DOGS OF ROME
THE RAIN FROM ALL THE ZONES OUT OF NOWHERE
THE UNCLE COMES WITH THE VEILED MONUMENT
OF THE NIECE WHICH THE WOODS ENTRUSTED TO HIM
THE MONUMENT IS A TORSO UNDER
THE AXE TWO SONS NUMBER THREE BANNED FROM ROME
AND A DAUGHTER HANDLESS BLOOD IN HER MOUTH
INSTEAD OF A TONGUE A HOWLING MASTERPIECE
THE COMMANDER CHANGES INTO A FATHER
HIS FLESH AND BLOOD INTO A WATERWORKS
THE NEGRO WATCHES THE ROMAN TRAGEDY
FROM THE WINGS OF HIS WORLD THEATRE
THE NEGRO WRITES A DIFFERENT ALPHABET
PATIENCE OF THE KNIFE AND POWER OF THE AXE

Titus.

TITUS   Hear me, Senators. You tribunes, stand
Out of pity for my age. My youth was
War, so that you here could peacefully sleep.
For all my blood, spilled in wars for Rome
For all the sleepless nights I spent in the frost
For these salty tears that you see here
Washing the furrows of my aged skin
Show mercy on my sons who are condemned.
No blemish, as they say, blackens their souls.
I would not cry for twenty-two sons if
They died in the lofty bed of glory.
For these here in the dust, tribunes, I write
My heart's grief with the tears of my soul.

107

Quench, my tears, the dry thirst of the earth
Before my sons' sweet blood stains it red with shame.
More rain, oh earth, will I pour upon you
Squeezed out of the two old holes of my eyes
Than does young April with its showers.
In the dry summer I'll be true to you
I will melt the winter's snows with warm tears
I'll paint your face with an eternal spring
If only you'll spare the blood of my sons.
Lucius with sword.
Worthy tribunes, noble old men of Rome,
Grant deliverance of my sons from death
Let me have my say, he who never cried
I ask you to give my tears a hearing.
LUCIUS   In vain, oh dear father, do you lament.
No tribune hears you, there's no one around
You are confiding your pain to a stone.
TITUS   Let me plead for your brothers, Lucius.
High tribunes, listen to me one more time.
LUCIUS   My father, no tribune hears what you say.
TITUS   It doesn't matter, man. If they heard me
They wouldn't believe me and if they did
They would be unmoved. Of course I must plead
Denuded of my pride, Rome, which was my pride
That's why I'm telling my pain to these stones
Which, although they cannot answer me
I prefer in a way to the tribunes
Because they do not interrupt my speech.
If I cry they capture the tears humbly
At my feet and thus cry along with me.
If they were dressed up in dignified robes
Rome would not have tribunes their equal.

A stone is soft like wax, stone-hard are tribunes.
A stone is mute and without malice but
The tongues of tribunes will talk men to death.
Why do you stand there with your naked sword.
LUCIUS   To preserve my brothers from their death.
The judges have already rewarded
My first try with eternal banishment.
TITUS   You're a lucky man. They showed you mercy.
Dumbbell, Lucius, how is it you don't know
Rome is just a jungle roamed by tigers.
The tiger rips in and Rome has no tooth
Except for me and mine. You're lucky too
To be banished from these cannibals.
What's this coming with our brother Marcus.
Marcus, Lavinia.
MARCUS   I bring you what will teach your eyes to cry
Or if you've no water left, your heart will break.
To your old age I bring consuming sorrow.
TITUS   It will eat me up. Let me see it then.
MARCUS   This was your daughter.
TITUS   Yes, Marcus, that she was.
LUCIUS   No, looking at this picture kills me.
TITUS   Weak-hearted boy, stand and look at her.
You, speak, Lavinia, what cursed hand
Displays you handless in your father's sight.
Who's the fool who pours water in the sea
And throws kindling onto the fires of Troy.
My misery reached its peak before you came
Now like the Nile it breaks down the dams.
A sword, I want to cut my hands off too.
They fought for Rome and quite in vain and
Creating life nurtured this misery.

I have held them high in childish prayer
They have served me for no use at all.
Now all the service I require of them
Is that the one will cut the other off.
Good thing, Lavinia, that you have no hands
Because hands that serve Rome do no good.
LUCIUS   Tell us, dear sister, who deformed you.
MARCUS   The tender instrument of her thoughts
Which once pronounced such pretty babbling talk
Has been ripped out of its beautiful cage
And sings no more, melodious as a bird
Sweet and changing, a joy to every ear.
LUCIUS   Then say it for her, who was it did this deed.
MARCUS   I found her this way, circling in the park
Quite like the deer that attempts to hide
The incurable wound before death.
TITUS   She was my doe. Whoever made this wound
Has hurt me more than if he struck me dead.
I am a man up on a high cliff
Surrounded by a wasteland of water
Look, how the flooding tide grows wave by wave
And always waiting for an envious swell
To swallow me into its salty bowels.
My poor sons follow the path toward death
Here stands my other son: he is banished
Here is my brother who cries my tears.
Here cries what cuts the deepest in my heart
Lavinia, dearer than myself to me.
Had I only seen a painting of this
It would have driven me to madness.
What should I do. Your living body like this
Before my eyes, no hand to wipe away

The tears, nor tongue to tell who tortured you.
Your husband is dead and for his death
Your brothers now also condemned to death.
Look, Marcus, my son Lucius, look at her
Tears as I mentioned your brothers' names stand
On her cheeks, like honeydew on lilies
Freshly plucked, and already withered.
MARCUS   Is she crying because they killed her husband
Or because she knows they are innocent.
TITUS   If they killed him, then you should be glad
Because the law has taken on revenge.
No no, they could never do such a deed
And push their sister deep into mourning.
Lavinia, let me kiss your lips
Or give me a sign how I can help you.
Should we all, your good uncle your brother
And you and I go sit by a fountain
And lower our gaze to look at our cheeks
Checkered like a field with the mud left behind
By a flood and we'll look in the fountain
So long that we have changed its clarity
Into a gray puddle with our salty tears.
Or should we cut off our hands and chew off
Our tongues to be like you and live the rest
Of our lives in pantomime. What should we do.
Because we still have tongues in our mouths
Let us imagine the misery to come
So that posterity can admire us.
LUCIUS   Father, save your tears because your pain
Makes my poor sister sob even harder.
MARCUS   Be quiet, my niece, Titus, dry your eyes.
TITUS   Oh Marcus, Marcus, brother, don't I know

111

Your handkerchief drinks away none of my tears
Flooded already with your own, poor thing.
LUCIUS   Lavinia, let me dry your cheeks.
TITUS   Look, Marcus, look. I understand her signs.
If she only had a tongue to speak with
She'd say to her brother what I said to you.
His handkerchief, soaked with his honest tears
Cannot serve to dry her cheeks of mourning.
What a pretty harmony of grieving cries
As far from help as the void from paradise.
Aaron.
AARON   Titus Andronicus, my lord and Caesar
Sends word to you: if you love your sons
Then Marcus, Lucius or you, old Titus
Or someone of your family should cut
Off your hand and send it to Caesar
Who in return will send you both your sons
Alive and that shall atone for their guilt.
TITUS   Oh merciful Caesar. Friendly Aaron.
Whenever did the raven bring to the lark
The news that the sun rises again.
With all my heart I give my hand to Caesar.
Good Aaron, will you help me cut it off.
LUCIUS   Wait, father, these your noble hands with which
You brought down so many enemies
Into the dust have no price. I offer
My hand. My youth has more blood than your age
May my blood save the lives of my brothers.
MARCUS   You both with four hands have defended Rome
And held high the bloody axe of war
Writing extinction on the enemies' front.
Yes, you are both pictures of your glory

Idle was my hand. May it now serve
To ransom my nephews from their death.
Then my hand was kept for a good purpose.
AARON   Well, make up your minds whose hand it will be
Else I fear they'll die before they're pardoned.
MARCUS   My hand goes with you.
LUCIUS   By heaven, it will not.
TITUS   Sirs, don't argue. A dried up herb like this
Deserves to be uprooted. Therefore, mine.
LUCIUS   Father, if I still count as your son
Let me preserve my brothers from death.
MARCUS   In the names of our father and mother
Let me show you what a brother's love means.
TITUS   Then you two must agree. I'll save my hand.
LUCIUS   I'll go get the axe.
MARCUS   But I will be the one to use it.
Marcus, Lucius exit. A hand from the audience.
AARON   The Negro thanks you for your helping hand
You'll need it to applaud in spectator-land.
TITUS   Come, Aaron, we will deceive them both
Lend me a hand and I will give you mine.
AARON   If this is called deceit, I'll be honest
Never in my life thus to deceive.
In another way I will deceive you
Which you will know in less than half an hour.
Aaron chops off Titus' hand. Lucius, Marcus.
TITUS   No more argument. What must be is done.
Good Aaron, give my hand to Caesar.
Tell him, it is a hand that protected
Him from a thousand dangers, ask him for
A grave for it, which deserved more. Let it
Have that. As to my sons, tell him they are

My precious jewels, purchased at a small price
And costly, since I bought what belongs to me.
AARON   I'll go, Andronicus. And for your hand
Expect to see your sons very soon
Their heads I mean. Even the foretaste
Of this trickery satisfies my hunger.
Let fools do good, and white mercy scream
Black as his skin will Aaron's soul gleam.
Aaron exits.
TITUS   Here I raise this one hand high to heaven
And bow to the earth the weak rest of me:
If there is any power that has a heart
For tears I call on it. You kneel with me.
Do that, my heart. Heaven, hear our prayers
Or we will breathe you gray with heavy sighs
And swallow your sun like a cloud of smoke
As it suffocates the light in its embrace.
MARCUS   Brother, speak of what is possible
And don't go into these deeper matters.
TITUS   Is not my grief deep and groundless
Then bottomless like it shall be my complaint.
MARCUS   Then let reason rule over your mourning.
TITUS   If there were such a thing as reason
In this misery I could contain my woe:
Does the earth not swim when heaven cries
When a storm brews, does not the crazy sea
Foam and threaten the firmament with its swell.
If you want a reason for this revolt:
I am the sea. Hear its sighs in the wind.
It is a heaven of tears, and I the earth:
Moved by its sighing is my ocean and
Delivered to the Deluge is my earth

Groundlessly swimming in the downpour of tears.
My bowels will not contain my misery
Like a drunkard I must vomit it out.
Allow me that. Losers must be allowed
To ease their stomachs with a bitter tongue.
A messenger with two heads and one hand.
MESSENGER Titus Andronicus, you are badly
Paid for the good hand you sent to Caesar.
Here are the heads of your noble sons
Here is your hand, returned to you with scorn
Your pain's their fun, your sacrifice a joke
It hurts me more to see your misery
Than to recall my own father's death.
Messenger exits.

DIGRESSION OF THE NEGRO ON POLITICS

THE EMPEROR SAYS IT WAS THE WRONG HAND
IT WAS THE OTHER ONE CAESAR WANTED
HOW CAN HE STEAL FROM YOU YOUR RIGHT HAND
WHICH HAS DONE SO MUCH FOR ROME AND FOR HIM
WHAT CAN YOU THINK OF HIM THAT HE WOULD ASK
YOU SHOULD AVOID LOOKING IN THE MIRROR
TITUS ANDRONICUS ROME'S NONCOMMANDER
SO THAT YOU STOP CONFUSING LEFT AND RIGHT
THE EMPEROR THANKS YOU FOR YOUR GOOD HAND
CAESAR DOESN'T NEED IT ANY MORE YOUR HAND
WHICH YOU CAN NO LONGER EMPLOY FOR ROME
AND TO REMIND YOU OF THIS LOSS WHICH YOU
INCURRED BECAUSE YOU LACK TRUST IN CAESAR
KEEP THE OTHER HAND SO JUST BECAUSE YOU'RE HANDLESS

LIKE YOUR DAUGHTER WITH HER STUMPS YOU DON'T
FANCY YOURSELF A BETTER SORT OF MAN
THE DAUGHTER TONGUELESS FOR HER CROWN
TO GET THE JUMP ON THINGS WHY DON'T YOU RIP
YOUR OWN TONGUE OUT NO EAR HEARS ITS WAILING
THE HEADS OF YOUR LOVED ONES FREED FROM THEIR NECKS
THOSE FOR WHOM YOU MARCHED ON YOUR KNEES THROUGH
ROME
WOULD YOU LIKE TO STROKE THEM WITH THIS BROKEN
HAND

SO THE DEAD HAVE DEADLY ENTERTAINMENT
SAYS CAESAR TO YOU FROM THE NEGRO'S MOUTH
TITUS   When will it end this terrifying sleep.
MARCUS   Enough of fine speeches. Andronicus, die.
You aren't asleep: here are the heads of your sons
Here your hand accustomed to war, and here
Your mutilated daughter, banished is
Your other son, deadened by this stony scene
Am I, your brother, cold and lifeless.
He will no longer deny your sorrows
Pull out your silver hair, with your teeth
Chew off your other hand. May this picture
At last extinguish sight from our poor eyes.
This is the time of the storm. Why don't you speak?
Titus laughs.
You're laughing. That's not what these times call for.
TITUS   If I still had any tears to shed.
And by the way: sorrow is my enemy.
How can I, if it conquers my eyes
And makes them blind with the tribute of tears
Go to find the cave where revenge lives.
Yes, these heads are talking to me and they

Threaten me, that I'll never find mercy
Until this infamy has been repaid
In cash in the throats of those who made it.
Come, let me see what my work shall be.
You, a people in mourning, close your circle
Round me, that I can turn to each of you
And swear that I will right each of your wrongs.
That is my oath. Brother, you take one head
In this hand I will carry the other.
Lavinia, you should join us too.
Here, my sweet one, hold my hand in your teeth.
And as for you, my boy, get out of my sight.
You are banished and here you can't remain.
Flee to the Goths, go recruit an army
And if you love me, as I believe you do
Kiss me and go, we have so much to do.
LUCIUS Farewell, Andronicus, noble father
No man in Rome knows greater grief.
Live, proud Rome, until I make my return.
I pledge to you more even than my life
Loving more what I leave than what I reap.
Live well, Lavinia, noble sister.
If only you were what you were before.
For Lucius lives no more, nor Lavinia
Except in hate and the hope of justice.
If Lucius lived, then to repay your wounds
You would see Saturninus and his lady
Eating dust under the columns of Rome
As once did old Tarquin and his queen.
My path is to the Goths and to power
Count your days, Rome. I am the night. It is my hour.

6

THE COMMANDER'S SON GOES INTO EXILE
A BASTARD OF HIS FATHERLAND A JEW
TWICE A BASTARD WHEREVER THE WIND BLOWS HIM
FOUR WEEKS LATER A GOTH WILL COLLECT HIM
ON THE STEPPES HALF TURNED INTO A BEAST
AND ROUGHLY DRAG HIM TO HIS CHIEFTAN'S CAMP
A dog or a Roman /
A Roman dog /
He barks Latin /
Soon he'll whine Gothic
Who are you /
Lucius Andronicus the son /
Of the butcher Looking for a quick death
We have time we're waiting on the snow
That blows us to Rome Rome can't run away
From us The cities stand still and Goths ride
No city rises from the beat of our hooves
Prepare yourself for a very long death /
I'm banished from Rome My father dishonored
I seek friends among the enemies of Rome /
You are a Roman Go wash his brain
IN THE VAPORS OF DRUGS THE SECOND BIRTH
THE MOTHER'S WOMB IS A TUB OF BOOTY
AND OUT OF THE WASH CLIMBS THE NEW ANIMAL
IN HIS HEART A STAKE WHICH SHARES ITS BEAT
LOYALTY DOESN'T MAKE THE WORLD GO ROUND
AND EVERY NEW DAY BETRAYS THE OLD ONE
THE BEST ENEMY OF THE RATS IS THE RAT
POISON AGAINST POISON ROME AGAINST ROME

LUCIUS ANDRONICUS GENERAL OF THE GOTHS
IN ROME THINGS ARE GOING THEIR OWN WAY
THEY WEAR CIVVIES THE DIURNAL EATS AND SHITS
ROME LIVES AND LAUGHS INCREASES UNDER THE AXE
TITUS ANDRONICUS SHREDS HIS OWN HIDE
WITH HIS TEETH HIS LEFT CLAW HIS RIGHT STUMP
THE COMMANDER'S UNIFORM FREEZES IN SHIRT
WHIPPED BY RAIN THAT IS FALLING UPWARDS
BEGGARS AND DOGS ARE SHARING THE SCRAPS
ROME SIGHS WITH RELIEF The vampire bleeds
THE COMMANDER REBUILDS HIS FAMILY
INTO A FIGHTING MACHINE FOR CIVIL WAR
HE THROWS HIS CHILDREN LIKE HAND GRENADES
WOUNDS ARE HIS WEAPONS EVERY STUMP A WIN
THE BATTLE IS CARRIED ON IN THE CLOUDS
AND WITH THE ARSENAL OF THE LIBRARIES
HE WHO HAS NO HANDS READS WITH HIS TEETH
NO WORD THAT THE NIGHT DOESN'T COLOR WITH BLOOD
ROME'S COMMANDER PRACTICES KILLING FLIES
MADNESS ESCALATES TO A WAR OF THE STARS
I want to turn the sky into a blood blister

7

Titus, Marcus, Lavinia, Boy.

TITUS   Well, well. Sit down. And see to it you don't eat
More than just enough to give us strength
To take revenge for this our bitter woe.
Marcus, untie these knots that bind you
To suffering. Your niece and I here are
Poor creatures: we're three hands short. Unlike you

We can't cross our arms to own our ten-fold
Grief. This orphaned left hand sticks around
To rule my heart which mad with misery
Booms in the hollow dungeon of my flesh
I knock it down thus.
You miserable landscape that speaks in signs
Can't you restrain it when your heart goes wild
And beat your breasts until it stops talking.
Injure it with your sighs, my little girl
And strike it dead with moaning, or take
A tiny knife between your teeth and dig
A hole right over your heart so that all
That is flowing from your poor eyes runs in
The pit and drowns the little whining fool
In tears that have the salt of the sea.
MARCUS   What, brother. Don't teach her to use her hand
Thus violently against her tender life.
TITUS   Say what. Has sorrow made you silly.
No, Marcus, brother, the madness is mine.
How would she lay a hand on her life and
Which hand. Why are you talking about hands.
So that Aeneas can lament again
How Troy burned and he was turned to grief.
Don't busy your hands with words and talk of hands
Until we've forgotten we have none.
How the fever criss-crosses my speech.
As if we could forget about our hands
If only Marcus would not say the word: hands.
Let's dig in. Come. Eat something, my dear girl
There's nothing to drink. Marcus, hear what she says.
I'll translate the signs of her martyrdom:
She says she drinks no other drink but tears

Brewed with her sorrow and served on her cheeks.
Speechless lamenter, I'll learn to read you
Until even your silence speaks to me
As Latin prayers speak to mendicant monks.
You shall not sigh or raise high your stumps
To the heavens, or wave or nod or kneel
Or make any other sign but I shall
Create from it an alphabet to learn
In speechless practice to understand you.
BOY   Grandfather, give up your bitter lament.
Make my aunt happy with a fairy tale.
TITUS   Quiet, my tender sapling, made of tears.
And tears will soon drown away your life.
Marcus, what do you strike at with your knife.
MARCUS   At this, my lord, which I killed: a fly.
TITUS   Shame on you, murderer, you killed my heart.
My eye is overfed by cruelty
The deed of death, done to the innocent
Doesn't suit my brother, I am Titus
Andronicus, who has seen too much death
Done to the innocent. Get out of my sight.
A murderer is no companion for me.
MARCUS   Brother, I only swatted a fly dead.
TITUS   Only. What if the fly has parents.
They would buzz their golden wings in mourning.
Poor harmless fly.
It flies hither, with its little humming
To make us happy, and you strike it dead.
MARCUS   Forgive me, it was black, like the Negro
Of the empress. That's why I struck it dead.
TITUS   Oh Oh Oh
No, pardon me, that I scolded you.

You have performed a merciful deed.
Give me the knife. I will slice it up.
Only a fly, that is only a Negro
Because it is black, like the Negro, let's
Butcher more flies, brother, more, more, more
Chop their hands off and cut out their tongues.
We've not sunk so low that we can't even
Slaughter a fly or a thousand flies or two
Together. The black ones like the Negro.
That is for you. That is for Tamora.
MARCUS The poor man. So entangled in his grief
He strikes at shadows instead of bodies.
BOY Help me, Grandfather, she's following me.
MARCUS Lucius, stand still. Why be afraid of your aunt
She loves you too well to do you harm.
BOY Loves me. Yes, when my father was still in Rome.
MARCUS What's she trying to say.
TITUS She is trying to say something.
MARCUS Stay, Lucius, don't be afraid. Remember
She read you poems by great Cicero
THE ART OF SPEECH, with no less love than Cornelia,
Mother of the Gracchi, had for her sons.
BOY Yes, and just like Hecubah of Troy she
Is crazed with suffering and that scares me.
TITUS Lavinia. Marcus, turn the boy away.
What are you doing with your stumps. Bad girl.
Who taught you to dance such a cheeky show.
Did you lose your sense of shame with your hands.
And better without hands than without shame.
What now, Marcus, what does she want with books.
Here is a book that she desires to read.
What is it, girl, boy, open it for her.

Read what you want, if it deadens your pain.
And may the heavens reveal to us soon
The damned perpetrator of this deed.
Why does she beat the air with both arms.
MARCUS   I think, she's saying, there was more than one
Who did it to her. Yes, there was more than one.
Or she pleads with heaven for revenge.
TITUS   Lucius, what's the book she's pulling on.
BOY   Ovid, Grandfather, the *METAMORPHOSIS*
My mother gave it to me.
MARCUS   Out of love for the dead woman
Perhaps she picked it out of the others.
TITUS   Quiet. How busily she turns the pages.
Help her. She wants what. Should I read, Lavinia.
That is the sad tale of Philomela
It tells of how Tereus betrayed her
And raped her. And rape, I fear, was the root
Of your misfortune.
MARCUS   Look, brother, look.
How she quotes the pages with her teeth.
TITUS   Lavinia, sweet girl, have you been used
Like Philomela, crudely, by force
In the deserted and pitiless forests.
Look, look.
Lavinia sings about Philomela. See Appendix.
Yes, there was a place like that, where the hunt was –
If we'd never hunted there and never –
Quite the same as written by the poet
Made by nature for murder and rape.
MARCUS   Why would nature build a forest like that
If the gods didn't enjoy tragedies.
TITUS   Give us a sign, sweet girl, we are your friends:

What's the name of the Roman who dared do this
Or has Saturninus himself mounted you
Copying Tarquin, who once left the army
To wallow in Lucretia's bed.
MARCUS   Sit, dear niece, brother, sit down with me
Apollo, Pallas, Jupiter, Mercury
Should inspire me so I can uncover
This betrayal. Brother, look here, look here
Lavinia. The sand is even here.
Write if you can like me. I write my name
You see, without the help of any hand.
Damn the spirit, who forced us to such arts.
Write, good niece, now bring into the light
What god wishes to be seen for revenge.
And may the heavens take hold of your pen
To inscribe upon the earth your suffering
So we will know who did it and the truth.
Oh, read, brother, what she has written.
TITUS   Stuprum. Chiron. Demetrius.
MARCUS   What, what. The randy sons of Tamora
Have carried out this black and bloody deed.
TITUS   Are you so slow, lord of the great heavens,
To hear and to see these horrible crimes.
MARCUS   Stay calm, dear brother, I know too well
That the writing on this earth says enough
To plant mutiny in the gentlest souls
And to arm children to protest it.
Kneel down with me, Titus. Lavinia, kneel
Kneel, sweet boy, hope of the Roman Hector.
And swear with me, just as Junius Brutus swore
With the suffering husband and the father
Of the virgin after Lucretia's rape

That by best advice we shall prosecute
Our deadly revenge against the Goths
And see their blood spilled or die in shame.
TITUS   That is certain now. I wish you knew how.
Chasing her cubs, you'll wake the old lady
And if she gets wind of you, watch out.
The lion she's entertaining on her back
Who licks her fur and rocks in her bosom
When he falls asleep, she does what she wants.
Stay away, Marcus, you're too young a hunter.
Go, get us a blackboard made of metal
And with a pen of steel inscribe their names
And preserve it. The northern wind will blow
Away like pieces of paper the sand
On which the Sybil has written her verdict
And where's our lesson. Boy, what do you say.
BOY   I say, my lord, if I were a man
The cowardly slaves under Roman yoke
Would not feel secure in their mothers' beds.
MARCUS   Out of you speaks your father who often did
Just what you're saying, with no thanks from Rome.
BOY   And, Uncle, as I live, I will do just that.
TITUS   Come with me to the arsenal, Lucius
I'll arm you. Then you will bring the empress' sons
Certain presents I will intend for them.
BOY   Yes, my dagger in their chests, grandfather.
TITUS   Not quite. I will show you a different way.
Lavinia, come. Marcus, watch over my house.
Lucius and I go to perform a play at court.
Titus, Lavinia, Boy exit.
MARCUS   Heavens, you hear the wailing of the just
And do not act and have no words to say.

125

Marcus, attend him in his madness.

His heart is more scarred by sorrows than

His enemies' swords cut in his dented shield.

Not revenge, but justice was he ever for.

Heavens, lend your lightning to his good war.

8

Aaron, Chiron, Demetrius, Boy.

CHIRON   Demetrius, the son of Lucius is here.

He has been sent with a message for us.

AARON   A crazy message from the crazy old man.

BOY   My lords, with all due humility

I greet your Honors from Andronicus.

And implore the gods of Rome to depose you.

DEMETRIUS   Thank you, dear Lucius. What is your news.

BOY   The news is that you have been found out

As rapists. If you would be so kind:

My grandfather has sent you with good reason

The best pieces from his arsenal

An offering to your honorable youth

The hope of Rome, he asked me to say that

And now I have, and hereby present you

With his gift, which you will need, and soon

You should be well armed and well prepared.

And so I leave you, you two bloody rogues.

Boy exits.

DEMETRIUS   Weapons. That is an honest enemy.

There's something written on the packaging.

Let's see. Hey. What are those.

CHIRON   Dead flies.

Aaron is right, the old man is crazy.
DEMETRIUS   He lost his head along with his hand.
AARON   Pardon me, my lords, it's addressed to me.
The black flies are meant for the black man.
We know what we think of each other
Rome's great commander and the lord of the flies.
CHIRON   What's that on the paper.
DEMETRIUS   A romance
About Tereus and Philomela. Listen
To how he loves her: "He drags her from the ship
Into a dark forest, confines her there
In a sheep's paddock and quiets his lust
Deaf to her screaming. Was that not love.
Listen to how he made her mute. When she
Whined for her father and yelled out what he
Had done to her and called the heavens to witness
In the delusion that they are occupied:
Aren't you ashamed to speak your misfortune
Out loud, he says, grabs her by the hair, pulls
Her arms around behind her back and binds
Them with the tatters of her dress. But she
Doesn't resist, rather she's obedient
In hope for speedy death she bows her neck
Under his sword, am I your murderer
He says, pulling her hair tilts her head back
Reaches in her mouth which he has just kissed
Takes hold of her tongue and cuts it out
The root twitches, trembling babbles on the ground
On which it spews blood for one long moment
Like the tail of a snake looking for the body
From which a deft cut separated it
In loneliness the instrument of her screams.

It tells how she pleased him again and again."
Has ever the like been heard in Rome.
A provocative gift from old Titus.
CHIRON   That's a piece by Ovid. I know it well.
I used to cry on my school bench over it.
But this Tereus wasn't very smart:
He left her her hands to betray him.
DEMETRIUS   And he ate his son baked in a pie.
AARON   There are smarter people around, one hears.
To be an ass can be a good thing
In the tiger's bite he's still saying yes.
A piece by Ovid. Provocative gift.
This joke smells of blood. Our empress, were she
At our heels, would doubtless applaud this
Comedy Andronicus plays for us.
But Tamora is hard at work with Caesar
The agriculture of making his heir.
My young lords, did not a lucky star lead
Us to Rome, foreigners, and worse, captives
And at the very peak of the mountain.
It did me good, that a Roman commander
Gave a Negro his hand before the capitol.
DEMETRIUS   He gave us what was dearer to him, his daughter.
AARON   Isn't he in the right, Prince Demetrius.
Have you not treated his daughter well.
DEMETRIUS   I wish we had a thousand Roman ladies
Equipped like her to serve our desires
All in a row.
CHIRON   A prayer after my own heart.
AARON   We still don't have your mother's amen.
CHIRON   She'd give it for twenty thousand ladies.
Let's pray to all the gods for our mother's labor.

AARON The gods won't help us. Pray to the devil.
Trumpets.
DEMETRIUS Why did Caesar order trumpets to play.
CHIRON To celebrate that Caesar has a son.
Nurse with black child.
DEMETRIUS Quiet, who goes there.
NURSE God be with you this morning.
And, my lords, have you seen Aaron, the Moor.
AARON More or less a Moor, depending on the light.
Here is Aaron, what do you want with him.
NURSE Oh dear Aaron, we are all done for
Help now or disaster will befall you.
AARON Woman, what's this caterwauling you're up to
What are you carrying, swaddled in your arms.
NURSE Something I'd rather hide from heaven's gaze
The scandal of our empress, Rome's disgrace.
She has delivered, lords, she is relieved.
AARON Of what office.
NURSE The office of labor.
AARON God give her peace.
What has he granted her.
NURSE A devil.
AARON Then she's the devil's mamma: lucky throw.
NURSE A tragic and black unlucky throw.
Here is the brat, ugly as a toad
Among those born white in our climate.
The empress sends him to you, your stamp and
Your seal, and she bids you to baptize him
A Moor using the point of your sword.
AARON Shut your mouth
Whore. Is black the weaker color. Ha ha
Thick stomach. A splendid bloom you are.

DEMETRIUS   Scoundrel, what have you done.

AARON   Something you can't undo.

CHIRON   What you have undone is our mother.

AARON   Scoundrel, I have done her, your mother.

DEMETRIUS   Thereby, you dog of hell, you did her in.

Curse her lechery, her disgusting choice .

Damn the breed of so black a creature.

CHIRON   It should not live.

AARON   It shall not die.

NURSE   Aaron, it must. The mother wants it so.

AARON   How so, sister, must it. No one but I

Shall serve as hangman for my flesh and blood.

DEMETRIUS   Come, tadpole, I'll skewer you with my sword.

Nurse, give it here and plant it on the point.

AARON   Not before this knife plucks your bowels.

Butchers. Do you want to kill your brother.

Now by the candlelight of Rome's heavens

That flickered shining as I made this boy

Here on the point of my sword will die

Anyone who touches my first-born heir.

I'm telling you, boys, not Enceladus

With his gang from the breed of the giants

Or Alcides, or the god of war

Himself shall take this prize out of my hands.

You rose-colored, half-hearted little boys

You are whitewashed walls, you are beer hall signs

Coal black is more than any other color

And subjugates itself to no other

Because all the water in the ocean

Will not wash white the black feet of the swan

Should he cleanse them hourly in the tide.

And tell the empress, I am of an age

To keep my own. Whether or not she approves.

DEMETRIUS   Would you thus betray the mistress of your bed.

AARON   My bed is my mistress. That's who I am:

A picture of my youth, which I prefer

To all the world, and against all the world

I will protect it, if dozens of you

Go up in smoke, or Rome crumbles to dust.

DEMETRIUS   This thing causes our mother endless shame.

CHIRON   Rome will spit her out for this monstrosity.

NURSE   In his anger Caesar will have her killed.

CHIRON   I am red with shame, thinking of the scandal.

AARON   That is the privilege of white beauty

The color of betrayal, that red shame

Reveals the secrets you hold in your heart.

This wee thing is made of different stuff:

Look, how the black clown laughs at his father

As if to say: old man, I am yours.

He is your brother, my Lords, and well fed

By the same blood that helped you into life.

And he is released into the light of day

Out of the same womb that held you captive.

He is your brother, your mother knows it

Although his face is stamped with my likeness.

NURSE   Aaron, what should I tell the empress.

DEMETRIUS   Use your brains, Aaron, decide what to do

All of us will follow your advice

Your child will be safe so long as we are.

AARON   Let's sit down and collect our wisdom.

My son and I remain at a distance

So your color won't rub off, turn his blackness

Red. Stay away. Talk at will of safety.

DEMETRIUS   How many women have seen this child.

AARON   That's a good boy, my Lords. If we're aligned
I shall be a lamb. But if the Moor's provoked
The mountain lioness is a house pet
The ocean is a puddle to Aaron.
So, let's hear it, how many saw the child.
NURSE   Cornelia the midwife and myself
And no one else but she who birthed it.
AARON   The empress, the midwife, and you yourself.
Two will learn not to speak, the third is missing.
Woman, can you count.
NURSE   One. Two. Three.
AARON   Go to the empress. Tell her, I say this.
He strangles her.
Eeek. Eeek.
What the piglet screams when it has been stuck.
DEMETRIUS   What does this mean, Aaron. Why'd you do that.
AARON   Your royal highness, this is politics.
If she should live, she is proof of our guilt
Like a long-winded babbling rumor.
And now hear my plan: not far from here lives
A compatriot of mine, he's an ass.
Just yesterday his wife bore a child.
His child is like you, as white as you are.
Go get it and give the mother some gold
Tell them both what has happened and how it
Will lift their child into the highest ranks
It will be seen as the heir of Caesar
Stepping into the shoes of my own child
To dampen the storm that now brews at court.
The child of an ass will become an ass
Which Caesar is too, so he won't notice
He'll spoil it as if it were his own seed.

Listen to me. I gave her her medicine
And now you must see to the burial.
The field lies close, and you are made of
Sturdy stuff. Get this done and don't waste time
And send the midwife to me right away.
She shall be the nurse's companion.
Then women can gossip as they please.
CHIRON   Aaron, you don't even trust your secrets
To the air.
DEMETRIUS   You take care of Tamora.
For that she is bound to you just as we are.
Demetrius, Chiron exit.
AARON   And now to the Goths, quick like a swallow
To stow away this treasure in my arms
And greet in secret friends of the empress.
Thick-lipped slave, come, I'll carry you away
Because you are the one causing the storm.
I will teach you to eat berries and roots
And curds and cream and to suck on a goat
To live in caves. That is how I'll raise you
So you'll be a soldier and commander.

9

Titus, Marcus, Boy, Publius, Caius and others with bows. Titus carries arrows with missives attached.

TITUS   Come, Marcus, come, cousins, here is the way.
Sir boy, let me see your archery:
Pull your bow all the way, then your arrow hits.
Terras Astraea reliquit. We are
Abandoned by the goddess of justice.

She is gone, Marcus, she fled away.
Sirs, take up your instruments. You sound
The depths of the oceans. Throw your nets.
Perhaps you'll get lucky and catch her
I fear that there is as little justice
In the sea as on dry land. But try it.
And you dig with your picks and with your spades
And bore a hole to the middle of the earth.
There, when you reach the region of Pluto,
I beg you, give him this petition.
Tell him, it is for justice and assistance
And it comes from me, old Andronicus
Battered by sorrow in ungrateful Rome.
Ah Rome. Yes, yes, I brought on your misery
When I gave the votes of the people
To him the tyrant who opposes me.
Go to work and pay attention that you
Don't let any ship of war pass unsearched.
This degenerate Caesar may have held her
In chains below deck and sends her away.
Look in the brothels perhaps he made her
A whore. And churn up the graves with your spades
So we can be certain that she is dead
And whistle our melody to her bones:
Justice
MARCUS Publius, doesn't it pain you
To see him gone crazy like this, your uncle.
PUBLIUS And that is why, my lords, it's our duty
To watch him carefully night and day
And to serve as friends to his moods until
Time heals him.
MARCUS Time. Time. His sorrow, my son is beyond

134

Any kind of healing except by iron.
Go to the Goths. For this ingratitude
A war of revenge will come upon Rome
And upon that traitor, Saturninus.
TITUS Now, Publius, now, my gallant friends
Have you flushed her out, our lady.
PUBLIUS No, your lordship, but Pluto bids us tell you
If you want revenge from out of his hell
He is ready to serve you. Our lady
Is sadly, Justice, is very busy
With Zeus in heaven, he says, or somewhere
So you will have to have some patience.
TITUS Devouring me by delays makes me ill.
Now I dive into the lake which burns below
And pull her by the feet out of the flames
Ah Marcus, we are the bushes, not cedars
The bones of the Cyclops are not ours.
We are clad in iron, steel up to the neck
But we bear the weight of more injustice
Than any Roman could stand. If justice
Dwells no more on earth nor in hell we want
To go to heaven and move the gods
To lend us this lady for our war.
Come now. Take arms. We want to shoot holes
In the sky. You're an excellent archer, Marcus.
For Jupiter your arrow. This one for
Apollo. For Mars, this is my arrow.
Here, boy, for Pallas Athena. This one
Is for Mercury. Here, Caius, for Saturn.
Not to be confused with Saturninus:
Don't shoot into the wind. I hope I didn't
Forget any of the gods. Titus has

A lot to think on. Shoot and hit your mark.

Be sure to stand where you have good cover

If justice should fall out of the sky

Or a god should do us the honor or

The heavens crash on Rome and Saturninus.

Oh I forgot. Let's change colors so that

The gods can recognize we are Romans

Since black is white and white is black in Rome.

Now, you are Romans. Change your color.

Titus paints himself black. The others do the same.

Now I know you. Now you are Romans. Shoot.

MARCUS   Into the courtyard of the palace, my lords

Our arrows should tickle the emperor's pride.

TITUS   Shoot, Romans, shoot. A good cue, Lucius.

The virgin has been shot in her womb.

MARCUS   I aimed a mile over the moon, Sir.

Lord Jupiter has received his letter.

TITUS   Ha, Publius, what have you done. Look there.

You shot the horn off the head of a bull.

MARCUS   That was the joke, my lord. Publius'

Arrow made the bull rage, he hit the ram,

And the horns fell off in the palace yard

And then whom should they fit but Caesar

Who wears them now.

TITUS   God give him joy in them.

Clown with a dead bird.

News, news from the heavens, Marcus, the mail.

Well, what a piece of news. Where are the letters.

Will I have it, will I have justice

What does Jupiter say, who rules above.

CLOWN   The one up there hangs. They just took him down again, sir.

Hanging starts next week. Negroes in Rome, that's what it's come to.

136

TITUS   What did Jupiter say, I ask you.

CLOWN   Jubitters? What kind of a drink is that. No offense meant, Mr. Negro: your cutlery is rusty, I'd rather eat myself. I ought to have known: The Negro has no sense of humor, he is too black. Should I drop my trousers? THE CLOWN LOSES HIS TROUSERS AND WINS / THE AUDIENCE. A blank verse. Again nothing.

I get it, they're playing a tragedy.

That is a tragedy.

I can cry too.

He cries.

TITUS   What, rogue, aren't you the courier?

CLOWN   No, sir, you're wrong, I cannot cure you.

TITUS   How is that, don't you come from heaven's father.

CLOWN   No, from my father's cock. I was on my way to the courts of law with my bird, it was foreseen as a bribe, the judge likes birds, a legal dispute between my uncle and someone from the court.

MARCUS   Well, sir, your bouquet is fitting for the court. Let him take his bird to Caesar as our bribe. Lord Saturninus is a collector of dead things.

TITUS   Tell me, can you lay a case before Caesar with decency.

CLOWN   No, sir, honestly, I've been indecent to decency all my life.

TITUS   Come here, fellow. And no more of your jokes.

Give your bird only to Caesar, and

You will have from me his duty to you.

Here's some gold for the trip. Give me a pen

Can you present a petition for me

With decency.

CLOWN   Yes, sir.

TITUS   Then this here is a petition for you. And once you get to him, at the first glance you must kneel, then lick his foot, then hand over the bird and keep a lookout for your reward. I will be on hand, sir. See to it that you do it properly.

CLOWN   I warrant it, sir. Just let me do it.

TITUS Do you have a knife. Come, let me see it.
Here, Marcus, wrap it up in our petition
So it will go straight to Caesar's heart.
When you have handed it over at court
Knock at my gate and tell me what he says.
CLOWN God be with you, sir, until I return.
TITUS I am the knife that slaughters heaven.
Heaven is full of blood. Soon it will snow.

10

ANATOMY TITUS ANDRONICUS
DIGRESSION ON THE DETECTIVE NOVEL

WHAT DRIVES THE GENERAL IN PEACETIME
IN HIS CELLAR SECRETLY AT NIGHT
WITH SPIDERS AND WORMS IN THE TORCHES' LIGHT
REPLAYS HIS BATTLES TASTES HIS VICTORIES
CHOKES ON THE AFTERTASTE OF HIS DEFEATS
REGURGITATES HIS DEAD COUNTS UP HIS SCARS
WHAT A CLAMOR OF AXES AND OF KNIVES
THE ROMAN LEARNS THE NEGRO'S ALPHABET
LEARNS THROUGH HIS LOSSES TWO HEADS UNBODIED
THREE HANDS MISLAID AND ONE TONGUE ROTTING
MUTE SOMEWHERE IN THE FOREST OUTSIDE ROME
HE HAS RESERVES ROME IS HIS BUTCHER'S STALL
JUST LIKE WITH CAESAR NOW FOR HIS WAR
IN A SECRET OPERATION HIS WOLVES SEIZE
THE OFFSPRING FOR THE GRAVEYARD OF HIS HEART
IN THE CATACOMBS THROUGH THE SHIT OF ROME
VILIFIED BY COMPETITION FROM RATS
GOES THE TRANSPORT OF THE COMMANDER

WITH THE HAND-AXE STUDIES EAGERLY
THE PARTS' CONNECTION BONE MUSCLES WEBBING
OUT OF WHICH THE ANIMAL IS MADE
THAT HAS SERVED HIM IN SO MANY BATTLES
AS THE RED CARPET ON THE PATH TO GLORY
BURROWS IN THE LABYRINTH OF THE BOWELS
LOOKING FOR THE SEAT OF SOULS WITH HIS KNIFE
What lives in us that whores lies robs and murders
PLUNGES HIS ARM STUMP IN OPEN BODIES
AND WRITES THE INVOICE ON THE WALL IN BLOOD
Two heads hands three add to that one tongue
Broken hearts five of those, the dead not yet
Counted, life in disgrace and in exile
Where is the key to open the abyss
If I had nature on my torture table
The bill would be due as long as grass grows
IRON DOES NOT BREAK THE SLEEP OF THE DEAD
PERHAPS FIRE WILL LOOSEN UP THEIR TONGUES
THE COMMANDER CHASTISES THE ASHES
INTERROGATES THE BONES SIFTS THE BONEMEAL
SPIDERS LOOK OVER AT HIM FROM THEIR WEBS
A FEW ARE DANCING IN THE WAVES OF SOUND
WITH WHICH THE CITY PROPOGATES HIGHWAY NOISE
SOMETIMES WHILE DANCING PLUCKING A FLY
I am your emperor Revenge is my bride
TITUS ANDRONICUS BATTLE LEADER
IN THE RUINS OF HIS ANATOMY
DREAMS THE CHILDISH DREAM OF HIS LADY
Justice AND WHEN HE CLOSES HIS EYES
HE CAN TAKE HOLD OF HER BREASTS WITH HIS HANDS
Justice AND HER GOLDEN PRIVATE PARTS
Justice AND REVENGE LIKE AN ECHO

THE ASH WHISPERS AND THE BONEMEAL SINGS
AND ABOVE AGITATED BY THE FULL MOON
THE DAUGHTER IS HAUNTING ROME HER HOME
FIGHTS HER FIGHT AGAINST THE BLACK AND WHITE
OF LITERATURE IT IS THE MURDERER'S PIT
THE VERSE IS RAPE AND EVERY RHYME A DEATH
SWEEPS THE BOOKS OFF THE SHELVES WITH HER STUMPS
BURNING CANDLES CLENCHED BETWEEN HER TEETH
APPLAUDED BY THE ORPHANED GRANDSON
BURNS THE LIBRARY ON THE PARQUET FLOOR
AND BATHES HER STUMPY ARMS IN THE FLAMES
MEANWHILE THE GRANDSON PISSES IN THE FIRE

11

THE EMPEROR AND EMPRESS IN THE RAIN
OF DEAD HEAVENLY BODIES SHOT DOWN
BY ARROWS OF THE WILD COMMANDER
RAIN MADE OF MARBLE STATUES AND THE STARS
SHIVERING UNDER THE CANOPY HELD
BY COURT LACKEYS WHO QUAKE IN THE FACE
OF FEAR AND JOY FEARFUL JOY AND JOYFUL FEAR
OUTSIDE SWELLING UP THE RUMBLING OF ROME
CAESAR PERCEIVES THE WORDS BEHIND THE TEXT
OF HIS OFFICIALS' FALSE TRANSLATIONS
AGAINST THE HEAVEN THAT SNOWS MONUMENTS
HANGED ON THE LAST ROPE THAT HOLDS IN ROME
THE CLOWN CONTORTS HIS LAST GRIMACE
FAR OFF THE HUNS' STORM THREATENS WITH ROCKETS
Saturninus, Tamora and others.
SATURNINUS   Look, my lords, what an attack. Has ever
A Caesar been toyed with in Rome like this

A Caesar so molested and maligned
Because he spoke the disinterested truth
A Caesar put out by his people with scorn.
You, my lords, know, as the gods know
Who have more power than you and are my shield:
Whatever these disturbers of the peace
Are spewing in your ears: nothing happened
Except the law applied to the stubborn sons
Of old Andronicus. And if and how
His sorrow has taken reason from him:
Should we fall victim to his lust for revenge
The bitter moods of his mental fevers.
Now he writes to heaven for assistance.
Look, this one to Jupiter, this Mercury
That to Apollo, that the god of war.
The message flies sweetly through the streets of Rome.
What, is it not libel of the senate
Our injustice painted on every wall.
A friendly humor, isn't it, my lords.
As if justice did not reside in Rome.
So long as I live, his pretend insanity
Shall not provide shade for his rage.
He shall know and his breed shall know that
Justice derives life from Saturninus' health
If she is sleeping, then he must wake her
So that her fury sharpens her axe
For the proudest surviving conspirator.
TAMORA   Merciful lord, my dear Saturninus,
Lord of my life, prince over all my thoughts
Calmly endure the errors of his age
Marks of the grief for his cheeky sons
Their death rips him apart and scars his heart

And better to make his hard yoke light
Than to chase down the worst or the best
To one he is this, to others he's that
For his silly hurt feelings. Tamora must
Shrewdly make everything right. But I struck
You, Titus, to the very quick. If you have
Bled yourself out and Aaron is clever
We are safe, our anchor in the harbor.
Clown.
TAMORA   Now my good man, what do you want. Speak to us.
CLOWN   Yes, with the tongue, if you Mistress are imperial.
TAMORA   I am the empress, but over there sits Caesar.
CLOWN   That one there? Goodnight from god and Franz Joseph. I
brought you a letter and my bird.
Saturninus reads the letter.
SATURNINUS   Go, take him away, and hang him on the spot.
CLOWN   I don't want a handout. How much money should I get.
TAMORA   Peasant, you shall be hanged.
CLOWN   Hanged. By the virgin, then I have made my neck stiff for a
worthy end. Perhaps the air is better up there. One cannot be hanged often
enough.
Exits.
SATURNINUS   This offense is repulsive unbearable
Should I be made to bear this monstrous spite.
I know where these scraps of writing come from.
As if his treasonous sons who are dead
According to law for the murder
Of our brother had been slaughtered unjustly
On my word. Drag the old man here by his hair.
No privilege for age or service.
For this mischief I'll be your slaughterer
Crazy fool, who helped to make me great

In the hope he would rule Rome and me.
Aemilius.
SATURNINUS   Aemilius, what news do you bring with you.
AEMILIUS   Arm yourselves. Rome never had greater cause.
The Goths are rising up, and now a force
Of stubborn men, who hunger for loot
Marches on Rome double-time, commanded
By Lucius, last son of Andronicus
Who threatens, in pursuit of his wrath
To wreak as much havoc as Coriolanus.
SATURNINUS   Lucius, the war hero general of the Goths.
I am bent to breaking, and my head hangs down
Like flowers in the frost, grass struck by storm.
Yes, now our worries are on the march.
It's he, the one the common people love.
I have myself heard them saying, when
I go around disguised as nobody
That Lucius' banishment was unjust
And they want him to be their Caesar.
TAMORA   Why this fear. Isn't the city secure.
SATURNINUS   Yes. And the citizens prefer Lucius
And follow him in revolt against me.
TAMORA   Think, as your name instructs you, as Caesar
Does the sun go dark when mosquitoes fly.
The eagle tolerates the bird's song
He doesn't care a whit what it means
He knows that the shadow of his wings
Can at his will quiet their melody.
That's what you can do to Rome's wavering men.
Brighten your spirit, and know, my Caesar:
I will bewitch the old Andronicus
With words sweeter and more dangerous too

Than bait to fish and honey-stalks to sheep.
The bait will drive the hook in the fish
And the sheep will turn mangy with sweet feed.
SATURNINUS   With us he will not plead for his son.
TAMORA   When Tamora asks him to, he will do it.
I can flatter him and clog his aging ear
With golden promises, even if his heart
Were impervious and his hearing dead
His ear and his heart would obey my tongue.
You go outside and be our ambassador.
Say, that Caesar wants to negotiate
With Commander Lucius, and set the meeting
In the house of his father, Andronicus.
SATURNINUS   Aemilius, do your task with dignity.
And if he wants security and insists
On hostages, ask him, who it should be.
AEMILIUS   With all my strength I will do as you say.
Aemilius exits.
TAMORA   I will go find Andronicus at home
And with my arts will talk so sweetly to him
That he will separate Lucius from the Goths
Now, sweet Caesar, be as cheerful as before
Bury your fear in my strategy.
SATURNINUS   Go then at once and sweetly flatter him.

12

Lucius, Goths, snow; later Aaron with the child.

LUCIUS   Tried and tested warriors, faithful Goths
I have received letters from great Rome
They speak of Rome's hatred for their Caesar

And how eager Rome is to see us there.
Great lords, be what your titles declare
Use your powers to end your dishonor
For every base deed inflicted on you,
Take thrice the vengeance.
FIRST GOTH   Fearless son,
Descendant of the great Andronicus
Whose name was our terror, now our comfort
Whose deeds and honorable fame in war
Rome thanklessly repays with contempt
Be bold with us: we go where you lead
Like murderous bees, when the summer glows
Who swarm down upon the fields of flowers
And revenge the treason of Tamora.
GOTHS   What he says, we say it also with him.
LUCIUS   I humbly thank him and thank all of you.
What kind of black piglet is that savage
Goth bringing, it walks on two legs as if
The offspring of a human with paws.
GOTH   Oh worthy Lucius. I walked away
From the army to see a ruined cloister
And so to brighten my heathen heart
And as I studied the crumbling building
I suddenly heard near a wall a child's cry.
If such a thing can be called a child.
I followed the noise and soon I heard
How a voice speaking stilled its crying:
Quiet, black slave, half me, half my lady
If your color hid your manufacture
If nature had given you your mother's look
You could have become Caesar, bastard
But where both bull and cow are white as milk

145

No coal-black calf has ever been bred.
Be still, kid, be still, he scolded the babe.
I will bring you to a Goth I can trust
Who when he knows you sprang from the empress
Will take you to his breast for the mother's sake.
At this, I drew my sword and jumped on him
In a surprise attack and dragged him here
So that you can deal with him as you'd like.
LUCIUS   Oh worthy Goth, that is the devil
In the flesh who robbed Andronicus of his
Good hand, the pearl that pleased the empress' eye
And here the dark issue of their sweaty love.
Cross-eyed slave, to whom did you want to give
The afterbirth of your hellish deformity.
Why don't you talk. Deaf. Not one word.
Soldiers. Go get a rope hang him from
This tree and next to him his southern fruit.
AARON   Don't touch the boy. He has the empress' blood.
LUCIUS   Twice as bad does not make him any good
Soon you will see Rome from high up, Negro.
Before my eyes close for good Rome will cease
Because it will be stomped by the boots of Goths
Because I want it Lucius Andronicus
A Roman
I want to see the whites of your eyes
When you give up the ghost, black as your hide
Bring a ladder for him to climb up.
First hang the child: he should see it twist.
To see a father mourn should not be missed.
Bring the ladder.
AARON   Lucius, save the child.
And take it to the empress from me.

If you do that I will show you wonders
That will advantage your campaign.
If you don't want that: then let the axe fall.
I say no more, may revenge rot you all.
LUCIUS   Say it and if I like what I hear
The child will live. I will have it raised.
If not, you'll have the view of Rome for free.
AARON   If you like it. I'm sure you will, Lucius:
To hear what I shall say will vex your soul
Or whatever you call that thing that you
Think gives you the advantage over us
Black nothings who frighten your pale courage.
I speak of murders disgrace massacres
Flesh-toned deeds and terror without end
Plots of disaster, treason and hate
Heard with terror and performed with rage.
And all that will be buried in my grave
Unless you swear to me the child shall live.
LUCIUS   Tell what you know, I say, your child shall live.
AARON   Swear that he shall, I'll begin right now.
LUCIUS   On what shall I swear. You don't believe in god.
If that's so, how can you believe an oath.
AARON   And if I do not believe, it's true, I don't
But I know you are full of religion
And have something inside you called conscience
With twenty priestly tricks and ceremonies
Which I've seen you're careful to observe
That's why I ask you to swear, for this I know:
A fool prays to an idol as if it's god
And keeps the oath that he swears by this god.
That's why I ask for it and why you should swear
Now before your god whatever that is

147

That you pray to and that keeps you afraid
Swear you will protect and feed and raise my child
Or I will come out of the void to find you.
LUCIUS   By my god, I swear to you that I will.
AARON   You know that I sowed this seed in the empress.
LUCIUS   The greediest and most depraved woman.
AARON   You know it. That was an act of mercy
Compared to what you are about to hear
It was her sons that butchered Bassianus.
They were the ones who cut out your sister's
Tongue and rode her hard and sliced her hands off
And prettied her up to look the way you saw.
LUCIUS   You call that prettying her up, Negro.
AARON   She was washed and clipped and prettied up
A pretty party for those who did it.
LUCIUS   Barbarians, beasts, villains just like you.
AARON   Yes, it's true, I was their coach and tutor.
Their wild sex drive they got from their mother
A trump card as sure as ever won the set.
The bloody stuff, I think, they learned from me.
A black dog will attack eye to eye
Let my actions be the witness for my worth:
I lured your brothers into the pit
Where the dead body of Bassianus lay
I wrote the little note your father found
I hid the gold that the letter mentioned
In service to the empress and her two sons.
And in all that was done to give you cause
To mourn I gave mischief my helping hand.
I played my faithless role to get your father's claw.
And when I had it, I stepped into the wings
And my heart almost broke from laughing.

I looked through the crack in the wall
When in exchange for his hand he got
The heads of his sons. I saw his tears and
I laughed so hard my eyes competed
With his to spew water. And then when I
Told it all to the empress she almost died
From joy to hear my happy news and paid
Me for my service with twenty kisses.
FIRST GOTH   Tell me how you can say that and not blush.
AARON   Yes, like a black dog, so goes the proverb.
SECOND GOTH   Do you regret any of these foul deeds.
AARON   Yes, that I didn't do a thousand more.
I curse the day, and yet I think that few
Of those I cursed escaped without some
Good dose of malice like killing a man
Or at least hatching his death, or disgracing
A girl or getting ready to do it
Blackening innocence with perjury
Planting deadly rivalry between friends
Taking care that the livestock of the poor break
Their necks, torching barns and haystacks at night
Riling the peasants EXTINGUISH WITH YOUR TEARS
Often I've dug up the dead from their graves
And planted them in front of their friends' doors
Just when the pain of death was forgotten
And with my knife carved in good Roman
Lettering in their skin as in tree bark
YOU MUST NOT LET YOUR PAIN DIE MY DEATH.
I have bestowed thousands of horrors
With an easy hand like one killing flies
And nothing hurts my heart except this:
That I can't bestow ten thousand more.

LUCIUS   A fast death is too sweet. Take it off his neck.

One doesn't hang the devil on the quick.

AARON   If there are devils, then I want to be one

A living torch in the eternal flame

I would like to have your company in hell

To tickle you with my bitter tongue.

LUCIUS   Stuff his mouth so that he speaks no more.

The Goths take Aaron off the rope and cram mud in the captive's mouth.

AARON   More. More.

I want to eat my way through half the earth

If I can only see, Roman, how your Rome

Turns to mud beneath the boots of your Goths.

Aemelius.

SECOND GOTH   There is a messenger from Rome.

LUCIUS   Aemilius.

Welcome. What is the news from Rome.

AEMILIUS   Lord Lucius

And through me to you, princes of the Goths

Greetings from Caesar, and since he hears

You are armed, he seeks to negotiate

At your father's house and you may name your

Hostages and they will be sent to you.

LUCIUS   What, negotiations at my father's house.

GOTHS   What does the general say.

LUCIUS   Do you have fathers.

GOTHS   And brothers, my lord, killed by Rome.

LUCIUS   Quite

Like your commander. And a sister too

Perhaps, robbed of honor by Rome and its Goths.

What should he say to this your general

He was a Roman and is not a Goth

When he closes his eyes he sees the city

The steppes see out of him when he opens them
He can only call the void his homeland
And his mother tongue is speechlessness
Homesickness is nausea and nosebleed
A chained dog strung up in the emptiness
Between two stars with equal gravity
A crazy crossing of projectiles and stars
This is your general what will he say
THE WASTING OF A SOUL THROUGH THE LANDSCAPE
No stone that stands on the other for a year
Sometimes the base of a column A hill Or
A stone that holds down a dead person
Horses are holes in time And sometimes
On the straight line between time and space
Face in the neck that is covered in arrows
Sirs let's ride down a bit of the future
We ride ahead we ride behind ourselves
Instructive Will you stay with us Roman.
GOTHS   We want to play with you Roman Stay.
THE COMMANDER KNOWS THE GAMES OF HIS GOTHS.
LUCIUS   Tell your emperor that you have seen me
Lucius Andronicus banned from Rome
I who was no Roman nor is a Goth
And feeds on stones and sand shits with Goths
Since Rome broke its best sword and threw it away
To have the breasts of a Gothic woman
Tell Caesar that he must place hostages
With both my uncle and my father
We shall come My dutiful Goths demand
Full payment in hand Give me your hand
So that you can also tell him that a Goth
Will take what has been given to him

His toy is the sword and not a speech
A GOTH CHOPS OFF THE ROMAN'S HAND WHICH
HE EXTENDS TO APPEASE THE COMMANDER
HE PUTS IT IN HIS POCKET A PIECE OF HOME
THE LAUGHTER DROWNS OUT THE AMPUTEE'S SCREAMS
When we're in Rome, I'll give it back to you
Just like Caesar gave my father back his
Hand it will be returned when we're in Rome
And Tribune take off that toga that kept
You warm when my father crawled on his knees
On the cold marble before the capitol
Would you help him out of his toga friends
He has only one arm.
THE GOTHS HELP
AND PEEL THE TRIBUNE LIKE AN ONION
GOTHS   We will turn you into a snowman.
LUCIUS   They want to know what you have underneath
They are hungry for knowledge my Goths
You have only one skin Why so stingy
THE GOTHS WATCH THEIR GOOD SNOWFLAKES MELTING
ON THE SKIN OF THE ROMAN UNTIL
THE BLOOD IS CLOTTED IN THE COLD SHIRT
THEY BIND TO A HORSE
GOTHS   It knows the way.
THE DEEP-FROZEN TRIBUNE AND CHASE HIM HOME
TOWARD ROME
GOTHS   Greetings to your empress.

13

IN ROME'S GOLDEN EVENING THE THEATRE
BLOOMS WITH DESIRE AND FEAR OF TRANSFORMATION

AND DEATH IN THE COLOR FILM OF DECAY

Tamora, Chiron, Demetrius.

TAMORA   In this foreign and frightful costume
I shall meet Andronicus. My role is
To play Revenge, which comes from below
In order to lend him a hand against
The injustice Rome heaped on its great
Commander. Here is his study. Where he
Lurks and mulls his vengeful plan for murder.
Titus, I am Revenge, I am your bride.
Let's invite your enemies to our wedding.
Titus.

TITUS   Who disrupts my thoughts. I know your trick:
You think, if you make me open the door
All my dreadful decisions will flee me
And my arduous work will turn to air.
You think wrong: what I've decided to do
Is written in blood here in front of my eyes
And what the text dictates will happen.

TAMORA   Titus, I have come here to speak with you.

TITUS   Not one more word. With the baton of one hand
How should I accompany my speech. You have
The advantage, madam, not one word more.

TAMORA   If you knew me, you would speak to me.

TITUS   If I were crazy. I know you well enough:
Witness the stump, witness this red writing here
Witness the furrows that my grief has plowed
Witness the red day and the night of lead
Witness my mourning, that I know you well
Empress Tamora, and your conceit.
Have you come to ask for my other hand.

TAMORA   Sorrowful man, I am not Tamora.

She is your enemy yes and I am your friend:
Revenge, sent here from hell to feed the vultures
Who are residing in your head next to feed
The vulture that lives inside your head
With revenge against your enemies.
Come and greet me in the light of the world
Speak to me of murders and of deaths.
Here there is no hiding place nor ambush
No distant darkness or murky hole
Where bloody murder and lusty rape find
Concealment for fear: I will detect them and
Say my name of terror in their ears: Revenge
Who teaches criminals to tremble.
TITUS   Are you Revenge and are you sent to me
To be the stake in my enemies' hearts.
TAMORA   I am, therefore come and welcome me.
TITUS   Do me one service, before I come to you.
At your side you have Rape and Murder.
Prove to me now that you are Revenge
And slit their throats or crush them beneath
The wheels of your chariot and I will be
Your charioteer and will pull you in circles
In a whirlwind round the globe. Get you
Horses black as pitch and speedy, and seek out
Murderers in the caves of their guilt.
And when your cart sways with their heads I will
Climb down and run along as a fifth wheel
Humbly as your servant all the day long
From its first appearance there in the east
Until it yields to night and dives in the sea
And day by day I shall give you service
If you crush Murder and Rape here into dust.

TAMORA   They are my servants and they accompany me.
TITUS   Are they your servants. And what are their names.
TAMORA   Rape and Murder, and they are called that
Because their task is to have revenge on
The doer of such deeds.
TITUS   They resemble the sons
Of the empress. And you look like her.
But we animals of the earth have eyes
Full of misery, crazed by delusions
Oh sweet Revenge, I come to you now
And if a one-armed embrace pleases you
Then I will embrace you as much as you want.
TAMORA   To approach him in this way feeds his madness
Whatever I write in his sick brain
Read it to him in everything you say
Because now he believes (and doesn't know it):
I am Revenge, and his superstition
Will deliver Lucius to us, his son
And while I beguile him at the banquet
I will pull from my sleeve a cunning trick
And divide the Goths against themselves or
At least make them an enemy to him.
He's coming, and I must play my role.
TITUS   I was too long in misery without you.
Welcome, fury, to my house of mourning.
Rape and Murder, you are welcome as well.
How you look like the empress and her sons.
You are welcome, only you are one Moor less.
Could not all of hell drive out such a devil.
Who ever saw the empress go out without
That black spot in her court. If you want to play
The empress to a tee it would be

Fitting that you had such a devil.
Welcome as you are. What shall we do.
TAMORA   What would you like us to do, Andronicus.
DEMETRIUS   Show me a murderer, I'll pay him back.
CHIRON   Show me a brute who has raped a woman
And my duty shall be to take revenge.
TAMORA   Show me a thousand who did you injustice
And I will be your revenge against them all.
TITUS   Look around you in the rude streets of Rome
And if you, dear Murder, find a man who looks
Like you, stab him to death: he's a murderer.
You, go with him, and if it happens
Dear Rape, that you find a man who looks
Like you stab him to death: he's a rapist.
You go with them: at the imperial court
There lives a queen, a Moor her shadow
You'll recognize her image as your own
Because she is you top to bottom, I ask:
Bring death to them both, a violent death.
They did violence to me and my own.
TAMORA   You have taught us well, what we shall do.
Would it please you, good Andronicus
To invite your thrice obedient son
Lucius, who leads a horde of warring Goths
To a banquet at your house. If he honors
You with his presence I will bring you
The empress and her sons Caesar himself
And all your enemies. They shall fall
To their knees to beg you for mercy
That you may open your heart to them.
What does Andronicus say to this plan.
TITUS   Marcus, sad Titus calls you.

Marcus.

Marcus, go to my nephew Lucius

You will easily find him by asking the Goths

Tell him to return to me and to bring

With him a few of the chiefs of the Goths.

Have him leave his soldiers where they camp.

Tell him, the emperor and the empress

Are dining with me, he should come join us.

Do that out of love for me as he should

If his gray father's life is of worth to him.

MARCUS   I shall do it and return with him.

Marcus exits.

TAMORA   I shall go and carry out the business

Of your revenge, my servants follow me.

TITUS   No, no, leave Murder and Rape with me

Or I will call my brother back again

And trust my revenge wholly in Lucius

And his swarm of Goths, eager for the downfall

Of Rome and its empress and her pups

Because they exchanged their furs for togas.

TAMORA   Sons, what do you say, will you stay with him

Until I tell Caesar my lord how I

Have set in motion the comedy

We are playing with the old man.

Humor his moods, be smooth, coddle him

And hang onto him until I return.

TITUS   I know you all, you think I'm crazy

I will hang them by their own noose

This pair of hell hounds and their old lady.

DEMETRIUS   Madam, go as you like, leave us here.

TAMORA   Revenge goes, Andronicus, farewell

To weave the net that your enemies will fell.

157

TITUS   I know what you're doing, sweet revenge. Go.
Tamora exits.
CHIRON   Old man, how shall we entertain ourselves.
TITUS   I have enough work for you to do.
Publius, come here, Caius, Valentine.
Publius and others.
PUBLIUS   What is your will.
TITUS   Do you know these two.
PUBLIUS   The sons
Of the empress, I think, Demetrius
And Chiron.
TITUS   Publius, what a mistake.
The one is Murder and the other is Rape
That's why you should tie them up, dear Publius
Caius and Valentine, take hold of them.
Often have you heard me wish for this hour
Now it is come, therefore bind them well.
Stuff up their mouths and silence their shrill cries.
Titus exits.
CHIRON   You dogs, take your hands off, we are the sons
Of the empress.
PUBLIUS   That's why we're doing
What was assigned to us. Stop up their mouths.
Is he tied up well too. Bind them tighter.
Titus with a knife, Lavinia with a bowl.
TITUS   Come, come, Lavinia, your enemies
Are bound, see, and already as mute as you
Their mouths stopped up. Do you two hear me well.
You dogs, Chiron and Demetrius
Here is the spring that you besmirched with shame
The summer, that you changed to winter.
You murdered her husband, for your misdeed

158

Two of her brothers died under the axe
My hand was cut off so you could have a laugh.
And her sweet hands, her tongue, and what is
Even more than hands and tongue, her virtue
You took by force, if you could still laugh.
What would you say, if I would let you speak.
We plead, dear Titus, please let us live.
Should I let them live, dear Titus.
I always wanted to see how a Goth
Looks inside out, dear Titus, and I say
To you now, that I will torture you.
One hand is enough to cut your throats
Lavinia holds the bowl between her stumps
Which receives your blood. You know your mother
Will be dining with me this evening.
She calls herself Revenge and thinks I'm crazy.
I am: I will grind your bones into meal
And make a dough of the meal and your blood
And out of this dough make fine pastries and
Out of your pretty heads I'll make a pie.
Extend your throats. Lavinia, come
Receive this blood, and when they are dead
We shall grind their bones to a fine powder
And mix it in with this sweet syrup
And in the pies we will bake their heads.
Come, come, you shall all serve as waiters
For my banquet, which I would like to be
Bloodier than the feeding of the centaurs.
TITUS ANDRONICUS THE ANATOMIST
CAREFUL HE DOES NOT DAMAGE THE FLESH
SLITS THE THROATS OF THE GOTHIC PRINCES
TITUS That whore, the unwashed thing you call a mother

Like the earth devours her own excretions.
This is my party, I invited her here
You are the banquet that fills her stomach.
Now into the kitchen. I'll play the chef
So that I can serve you to your mother.
Go and get me my last uniform.
TITUS ANDRONICUS THE PIONEER
OF NOUVELLE CUISINE: PERSON TO PERSON
THE HATE GOES LIKE LOVE THROUGH THE STOMACH
THE TRUTHS IN COOKING: PEOPLE ARE PEOPLE
PEOPLE EAT PEOPLE THEY MARCH INTO
THE LAND OF THE DEAD IN FORMATION
THE MOTHER SERVES AS GRAVEYARD. THAT SAVES GRAVES.

14

FAMILY GATHERING ROMAN SUPPER
THE GENERAL A NEW JESUS SHOWS
TO THE DINOSAURS THEIR FINAL FUTURE
THEN HUNGER STANDS IN THE DOOR BLACKENED
BY SWARMS OF FLIES OUT OF THE GOTHIC STEPPES
GRASS GROWS ON THE DATA BANKS RUST CHEWS
THE MACHINE PARK THE SANITARY LANDFILLS
SPICE UP THE EVENING MEAL WITH THEIR POISONS
THE DEAD CLIMB OUT OF THE SHIT OF ROME
Lucius, Marcus, Goths with Aaron, captive.
LUCIUS   It is not love that drives me toward Rome
I am in Rome because my father calls
GOTHS   We are here too and soon Rome shall know why
LUCIUS   And take care that our backs are well covered
I am afraid that Caesar is cooking
Up trouble We will plant the Negro here

To display him to his empress a black
Monument to her life of depravity
We want to put on a play for you
Negro and you should applaud at the end
This is your judgment chest-deep in the earth
Until the flies eat you and the dogs or
Whatever else is your equal below ground
To make it easy for them to find you
We will write the names of our dead in your hide
You are a good memorial red on black
Du you want to write the names on him Goth
GOTH   I can only kill, my lord, with my sword
LUCIUS   Soon enough you will learn how to write
This is for Martius This is for Quintus
Titus Andronicus the living dead
Lavinia buried mute in her body
The flies will come to read my writing
And tickle the names into your memory
Remember them before you forget it all
AARON   Before you have forgotten black Aaron
The sky of Rome shall be black with flies
This Aaron declares
MARCUS   Lucius kill him now
LUCIUS   Not yet Caesar it appears has arrived
Saturninus, Tamora, Aemilius and followers.
SATURNINUS   What Does the sky have more than one sun
I think Caesar is holding court in Rome
LUCIUS   What good does it do to call yourself a sun
And you don't know what happens under the moon
TAMORA   Half a Negro Who planted that here
LUCIUS   In Rome the Negroes grow out of the ground
TAMORA   And much shorter than someone here in Rome

161

Who lost his hand by folding it in prayer
LUCIUS   Do you know this Negro pretty empress
TAMORA   I knew a Negro He was black and so
Is this one A Negro is a Negro
MARCUS   Rome's Caesar Nephew Stop your quarrel
The Andronici invite you to our banquet
The meal is ready which the faithful Titus
Has prepared for us to the best of ends
Please take your seats
SATURNINUS   With pleasure Marcus
Titus as the cook, Lavinia veiled.
TITUS   Welcome Caesar Noble empress of Rome
You brave Goths Lucius my son welcome
You brought your father a present I see
For dessert a Negro I like it
The flies are collecting around their lord
How is your black constitution Negro
A poor meal but it does fill up the stomach
Eat eat
SATURNINUS   Andronicus why the uniform
TITUS   Your highness Rome's commander has become
A cook to entertain you and the empress
TAMORA   Good Andronicus it entertains us
TITUS   If you could have one look in my heart
It would entertain you more your highness
My heart's Caesar do you want to play with me
TAMORA   The old man's crazy Let him do what he wants
SATURNINUS   How does your game go Andronicus my dear
TITUS   It is a question game Heart or sting
SATURNINUS   Heart or sting your game seems crazy to me
TITUS   Yes like my head I will ask you a question
SATURNINUS   Ask what you'd like

TITUS   Thank you your highness
Then I will ask you a second question
SATURNINUS   A strange game What is the joke commander
TITUS   You wait to answer the first question
Until I have asked you the second question
The answer I'll bet will be the same to both
That is the joke You will laugh until you cry
SATURNINUS   Good let's bet
TITUS   The lives of our loved ones
Are you eating too empress
TAMORA   My hunger lauds the chef
TITUS   The meal praises you
SATURNINUS   The bet is on The lives of our loved ones
Now the question
TITUS   Are you eating empress
Did Virginius do right when suddenly
With his own hand he stabbed his daughter to death
Because her honor was taken by force
Would it be wrong if Caesar killed his wife
Because she had taken his honor
SATURNINUS   Andronicus your madness makes you drift
TAMORA   The old man's crazy
SATURNINUS   Yes he did right
TITUS   The reason Caesar tell me your reason
SATURNINUS   They should not survive their dishonor
Woman or daughter and renew the sorrow
Of Caesar and her father by their life
TITUS   The bet has been won and it has been lost
Lavinia you have earned your death
If I could stand in your skin before my sword
THE FATHER WITH HIS EYES CLOSED DRAWS BACK
THE VEIL FROM THE RUIN OF HIS DAUGHTER

HE SEES HOW SHE STANDS NAKED AND NEW
THE LAST EMBRACE ONE ARM LEFT A STUMP
THE BLIND ONE WITH HIS REMAINING LEFT STABS
THE KNIFE INTO THE DREAM THAT ROBS HIM OF SLEEP
Titus kills Lavinia.
AARON   Titus I call that a good sting
SATURNINUS   What are you doing misbegotten monster
TITUS   The bet is on The lives of our loved ones
She was my dearest and blind with tears
I have murdered the source of my tears
On your word after Virginius' example
Just as by my example on your word
Tadpole you will kill the source of your tears
Which you have not yet cried and your dearest
When you come to learn what you do not know
You whom I against Rome called to be Caesar.
TAMORA   Oh dear Saturninus give me your sword
And let me kill this monstrosity
Who poisons your ears with his wild speech
SATURNINUS   You could hurt yourself my dear empress
What is it I don't know What will I learn
Why did you kill your daughter yourself
Did someone rob her of her honor Who
TITUS   One thing at a time tree frog It wasn't I
Who first caused my daughter's blood to flow
Are you eating too empress eat more please
Demetrius and Chiron it was
Who raped her and who sliced off her tongue
And cut from her these lovely branches
SATURNINUS   Is that why they aren't here at the banquet
Where are they Bring them here this instant
TAMORA   I haven't seen either of them since dawn

TITUS   Then you must have weak eyes They are here
And you have eaten them you Negro-whore
How do they taste your scum
SATURNINUS   Negro-whore Who
THE GOTH QUEEN EATS WITH A NEW HUNGER NOW
TAMORA   Do I have you back with me my boys
AND SALTS WITH HER TEARS THE DEAR SUPPER
AARON   Oh Tamora Oh flower of my life
TITUS   Do you hear the animal who did your work
In your bed
LUCIUS   That is the fruit my Caesar
The Goths throw the dead child on the table.
Empress how do you like your black prince.
AARON   My fat bastard come I will kiss you to death
Aaron cries.
TITUS   The animal has tears that's how our game goes
Heart or sting
THE FROG WANTS TO TURN INTO A BLOODHOUND
HIS GAZE BLIND WITH TEARS FOR THE FIRST TIME
BIDS FAREWELL TO THE BREASTS OF THE GOTH QUEEN
SATURNINUS   Did you eat what was dearest to you
Eat your bastard too you love him more
He has the color of your heart Eat
My knife will be your dessert Negro-whore
TITUS   I am the cook And this is my wedding
THE COMMANDER WITH THE KNIFE OF THE CUCKOLD
BLOWS HIS KISSES TO HIS GOTHIC QUEEN
TITUS   And now the hour has come Tamora
I am your Caesar Revenge is my bride
Titus kills Tamora.
SATURNINUS   Payment for your last labor commander.
Saturninus kills Titus.

LUCIUS   This is for the emperor from the son
Of the commander returned home from exile
Lucius kills Saturninus.
That was decreed by the power of the breasts
Spits on Tamora.
No rooster in Rome crows for them now
*Romans draw their swords against Lucius, the Goths against the Romans. Lucius
takes the crown off dead Saturninus and puts it on.*
EXCEPT IN HIS GRAVE BY DEATH FORGOTTEN
A NEGRO HIS VOICE COMES FROM THE WORLD
WHERE DESERTS AND THE GLACIERS GATHER
FOR THE MARRIAGE OF THE PLANETS TO THE VOID
AARON   Let me see her one more time Uncover her
GOTHS   Do you raise your sword against your Caesar
ROMANS AND GOTHS   Hail Lucius Hail the new Caesar of Rome
THE COMMANDER'S SON RIPS THE CLOTH OFF
THE TABLE BOWLS AND GLASSES CLINK GOBLETS BREAK
AND THE BONES OF GOTHS ROLL IN THE SAND
GNAWED CLEAN BY THE ROMANS AND THE GOTHS
AND AMONG THE WINE AND BLOOD A BLACK PRINCE
HIS OBITUARY HIS FATHER'S LAUGHTER
LUCIUS   Rome's Emperor thanks ungrateful Rome
Go bury the dead and come mourn with us
What befell the Andronici No lament
For Tamora the tigress nor a grave
Set her outside for the dogs and birds
Birds and dogs will have to do her mourning
Leave the black dog where he's planted in the earth
To you my brave and loyal Goths our thanks
You are released back to your home in the steppes
Uncle, take care they go back well rewarded
GOTHS   Perhaps we like it here and want to stay.

LUCIUS   Rome has swords enough to drive you out
Laughter of the Negro, blackout.
WHILE THE NEGRO GROWS WHERE PLANTED IN THE EARTH
TRANSFORMED SLOWLY BY WORMS FROM THE DEEP
INTO DUST WHICH COLLECTS INTO DESERT
AND GROWS OVER ROME
THE GOTHS ATTACK THE CAPITAL OF THE WORLD
WITH STORMS OF ARROWS ON THE SOUTHERN CROSS
APPLAUDED SILENTLY FROM THE MASS GRAVES
IN THE GRINDING SPADES OF ARCHAEOLOGY
THE KNIFE CELEBRATES ITS MARRIAGE TO THE WOUND
IN THE CANNIBAL LOOK OF GOTH BUTCHERS
DANCES WITH THE NEGRO ON ROME'S ASHES
SLOW FOXTROT PAINTS THE SKY GRAY IN RHYTHM
WHICH BELOW APPEARS BLACK AND GROUNDLESS
UNTIL WHISTLING OVER THE LAST HAPPY END
THE WORLD TRAP SHUTS OVER THE FIRMAMENT

END OF PLAY

Appendix

I

In the Bochum premiere in February 1985, additional texts were used in the 3rd, 7th, 8th scenes.

In the 3rd scene: "Edward," a Scottish folk song, in the translation by J.G. Herder.

Your sword, why is it so red with blood? Edward, Edward!
Your sword, why is it so red with blood, and you come sadly here?—Oh!
Oh I have struck my hawk dead, Mother, Mother!
Oh I have struck my hawk dead, and I have none other like it—Oh!
Your hawk's blood is not so red, my son, confess to me—Oh!
Oh I have struck my red steed dead, Mother, Mother!
Oh I have struck my red steed dead, which was so proud and true——Oh!
Your steed was old and you aren't in need, Edward, Edward!
Your steed was old and you aren't in need, you have some other pain—Oh!
Oh I have struck my father dead, Mother, Mother!
Oh I have struck my father dead, and sorrow fills my heart—Oh!
And what penance will you do? Edward, Edward!
And what penance will you do? My son, confess to me—Oh!
My foot should not rest on earth, Mother, Mother!
My foot should not rest on earth, I will go away across the sea—Oh!
Oh what should become of your farm and home? Edward, Edward!
And what should become of your farm and home, so grand and handsome—Oh!
I'll let them stand 'til they sink and fall, Mother, Mother!
I'll let them stand 'til they sink and fall, don't want to see them again—Oh!
And what should become of your wife and child? Edward, Edward!
And what should become of your wife and child? When you cross the

sea?—Oh!
The world is large, let them beg in it, I'll see them nevermore—Oh!
And what will you leave to your dear old mother? Edward, Edward!
And what will you leave to your dear old mother? My son, tell me—Oh!
Curses will I leave you and fires of hell, Mother, Mother!
Curses will I leave you and fires of hell, since you, you told me so—Oh!

In the 7th Scene: "Lavinia sings of Philomele"

Away from the ship
In a gloomy forest
He quiets his desire
As she whines for her father
And calls on the heavens in the madness
That someone dwells there
Am I your murderer says he
Grabs her tongue cuts it out
The root twitches on the ground
On which she spits blood.

In the 8th Scene: The Digression about the Negro" etc.

Part of an essay by Gustav Sievers, from the Prinzhorn Collection, a collection of pictures, sculptures and texts from psychiatric facilities. The question
may arise, what is a Negro? And the answer follows: Is a Negro something
comprehensible, thus a rodent is something better known and it can be black,
therefore it is called that: seeing black rodents. But that would be mistaken.
This black rodent is blind, and if we can see him, he cannot see us, and thus
the viewing of blacks in our zone, as far as they are members of our own world
here, is impossible; they would be able to see us in that case. Now be careful
that the mole never sees the light of day. He is born below our level, lives and
dies under it, without seeing it or walking on it. In this form of life we can

recognize a Negro world that is contemporary with us in this zone. . . . the belief in a life in another and better world dates from the time when the parts of the world were not yet bound to each other, when they knew nothing of each other.

II

Unity of the Text

The commentary, as a means of bringing the reality of the author into play, is drama and should not be delegated to a narrator. It can be spoken as a chorus; by the actors playing the specific character to which it refers; by another actor playing a different character, who stands in this or that relationship to the character referred to or has no relationship at all. The expression of emotion can, as in Japanese theatre, be performed by the commentator (whether chorus or speaker); a report on the effect that it had by the actor. The repertory of roles (positions) that the commentary presents (spectator voyeur overseer reporter lecturer prompter agitator sparring-partner mourner shadow Doppelgänger spirit) are available to all who are part of the play. For each player the emotion that the text articulates/conceals can be set aside/acted out. No monopoly on roles masks gestures text, the use of epic theatre devices-no privilege: each has the chance to be alienated from himself. The Titus commentary plays with accidental material, the field of play is temporary, the coordinates are fear and geometry. (The real thing starts when the terror of day explodes the coordinates.) The theatricalization of reality by politics as dependence of technology, returns theatre to its reality, whose timing is the delayed explosion. The cancerous path of life in capitalism, as well as the coexistence with it on the common basement planets (it flies to the surface, in the basement death grows), destroys the connection of the actor to private property/his private property: he doesn't play a role any more. Dispossessing/freeing the actor as a condition of survival for the theatre. The bodies the compass needle: gesture measures its functions (blood pressure temperature) in the unfamiliar landscape, which is perhaps a landscape beyond death, or a place on the threshold. The text as knife, which loosens the tongues of the dead under the microscope of anatomy; theatre writes path marks in the blood swamp of ideas. If the role of leader of the dead is given to the commentator, the learning process of the dead must be shown, death as assignment, DISMEMBER REMEMBER, lesson, which must be learned, training for the resurrection (be it from the press against the idiots of criticism). In the bowels of tragedy, farce lingers, a virus from the future. If it explodes the larva, blood flows instead of sawdust. Death as embryo (the message of Ibsen). Or the other way around: God is the zombie, who brings the messiah to the world, his death as a condition of his birth. For the display of amputations and deaths, monuments can be used, bigger or smaller than life-size, on which the condition of the devastation will be marked, feed for the new animal, who populates the audience, in a rush to replace the human, or information for visitors from the universe, a message in a bottle, for happier galaxies, theatre as midwife of archaeology: the actuality of art is tomorrow.

Shakespeare a Difference

The attempt to write about Shakespeare, between Berlin, Frankfurt, Milan, Genoa. With the growing pile of notes the horror of its wording grows. Closest to Shakespeare in Genoa, at night in the medieval inner city and near the harbor. Narrow alleys—during the Middle Ages they were barricaded with iron chains against the people—between the palaces of the city-state's aristocracy, the Dorias, for instance, who have been made popular by Udo Lindenberg. On a wall the sprayed graffiti WELCOME TO HELL NO PITY HERE.* All this is like the way to the Globe* as Giordano Bruno described it, past taverns, brothels, and dens of cutthroats. Memories of the first reading: *Hamlet* from the school library, defying the teacher's warning to the thirteen-year-old about the original's difficulty. A black leather-bound volume, on the title page the stamp of the former grand-ducal grammar school. I imagined more than I understood, but the leap creates the experience, not the step.

The play itself is an attempt to describe an experience that has no reality in the time of its description: An end game at the dawn of an unknown day. BUT LOOK THE MORN IN RUSSET MANTLE CLAD / WALKS O'ER THE DEW OF YON HIGH EASTERN HILL. Nearly four hundred years later another version: IN RUSSET MANTLE CLAD THE MORN WALKS O'ER / THE DEW THAT GLISTENS FROM ITS STEPS LIKE BLOOD.

In between, there is for my generation the long march through the hells of Enlightenment, through the bloody swamp of the ideologies. Hitler's geographical lapsus: genocide in Europe instead—as usual and today's practice as it was yesterday's—in Africa Asia America. The St. Vitus's dance of dialectics during the Moscow trials. The lidless view at the reality of the labor and extermination camps. The village-against-city-utopia of the Hegel-reader and Verlaine-lover Pol Pot. The belated Jewish vengeance upon the wrong object, a classical case of belated allegiance. The lockjaw of a party, once beaten into the victor's role, when it is exercising its bestowed or force-fed power in the shortage-ridden economy of a Real Socialism. THE SCARS CRY OUT FOR

172

WOUNDS AND THE POWER / HAS COME UPON THEM LIKE A HEAVY BLOW. The clinch of the Revolution and Counterrevolution as the basic pattern of the century's mammouth catastrophes.

Shakespeare is a mirror through the ages, our hope a world he doesn't reflect anymore. We haven't arrived at ourselves as long as Shakespeare is writing our plays. The opening line of *Miranda's Song** from Auden's commentary on *The Tempest: My Dear One is Mine as Mirrors are Lonely** is a Shakespeare metaphor that is reaching beyond Shakespeare. NO MORE HEROES! NO MORE SHAKESPEAROS* goes the refrain of a Punk song. A fragment by Hölderlin describes the unredeemed Shakespeare: FIERCELY ENDURING IN THE FEARFUL ARMOR MILLENNIA. Shakespeare's wilderness. What is he waiting for, why in armor, and how much longer.

Shakespeare is a mystery, why should I be the one who betrays it, assuming I would know it, and why in a Weimar so distant from Shakespeare. I accepted the invitation and stand now before you, sand in my hands that's trickling through my fingers. *Hamlet* is an object of desire for critics. For Eliot the Mona Lisa of literature, a botched play: the remnants of the revenge tragedy—a marketable genre of the age as today the horror film—are butting awkwardly into the new construct and impede Shakespeare's material in its unfolding. A discourse that is broken by silence. The dominance of the soliloquies is no accident; Hamlet has no partner. For Carl Schmitt a text that is consciously confused and obscured for political reasons, begun during the rule of Elizabeth, concluded after the first Stuart assumed power, son of a mother who had married the murderer of her husband and died under the axe, a Hamlet figure.

The invasion of the times into the play constitutes myth. Myth is an aggregate, a machine to which always new and different machines can be connected. It transports the energy until the growing velocity will explode the cultural field. The first hurdle during my reading was Horatio's surprising speech, surprising from the mouth of a Wittenberg student, after the dead man's entrance at the coast of Elsinore. IN THE MOST HIGH AND PALMY STATE OF ROME / A LITTLE ERE THE MIGHTIEST JULIUS FELL / THE GRAVES

STOOD TENANTLESS AND THE SHEETED DEAD / DID SQUEAK AND GIBBER IN THE ROMAN STREETS / AS STARS WITH TRAINS OF FIRE AND DEWS OF BLOOD / DISASTERS IN THE SUN AND THE MOIST STAR / UPON WHOSE INFLUENCE NEPTUNE'S EMPIRE STANDS / WAS SICK ALMOST TO DOOMSDAY WITH ECLIPSE … History in the context of nature. Shakespeare's view is the view of the epoch. Never before did interests appear so naked, without the drapery, the costume of ideas. MEN HAVE DIED FROM TIME TO TIME AND WORMS HAVE EATEN THEM BUT NOT FOR LOVE. The dead have their place on his stage, nature has the right to vote. That spelled in the idiom of the nineteenth century, which still is the idiom of conferences between the rivers Oder and Elbe. Shakespeare had no philosophy, no understanding of history: his Romans are of London.

Meantime the war of the landscapes, which are working toward the disappearance of Man who has devastated them, isn't a mere metaphor anymore. Dark times, when a discourse about trees was nearly a crime. The times have become brighter, the shadows fade out, it's a crime to be silent about trees. The horror that emanates from Shakespeare's mirror images is the recurrence of the same. A horror that drove Nietzsche, the God-forsaken reverend's son, from the misery of the philosophies into his dance of knives with the ghosts from the future, from the silence of the academies onto the white-hot high wire of history, stretched BY AN IDIOT FULL OF SOUND AND FURY* between TOMORROW AND TOMORROW AND TOMORROW.*

The accent is on the *AND*, the truth is a steerage passenger, the abyss is the hope. Vasily Grossman has Stalin—the Meritorious Murderer of the People, as Brecht once called him—see in the German tank turrets moving towards Moscow a thousand times the murdered Trotsky, Creator of the Red Army and Executioner of Kronstadt. A Shakespeare variant: Macbeth sees Banquo's ghost, and a difference. Our task—or the rest will be statistics and a matter of computers—is the work at this difference. Hamlet, the failure, didn't accomplish it, this is his crime. Prospero is the undead Hamlet: after all, he smashes his staff, a reply to the new Shakespeare reader Caliban's topical rebuke to all hitherto existing culture:

YOU TAUGHT ME LANGUAGE AND MY PROFIT ON'T
IS I KNOW HOW TO CURSE.

About the Translators

Carl Weber is a director and translator who early in his career worked as an assistant director to Bertolt Brecht and actor at the Berliner Ensemble. He has directed plays in major theatres in the U.S., Europe and Canada. Weber has also translated the work of Peter Handke, Franz Xaver Kroetz and several PAJ Publications titles by Heiner Müller, including *Hamletmachine and Other Texts for the Stage, Explosion of a Memory* and *The Battle.* He is Professor Emeritus in the Department of Theater and Performance Studies at Stanford University.

Paul David Young is a recipient of the Kennedy Center's Paula Vogel Playwriting Award. His plays have been produced at MoMA PS1, Marlborough Gallery, the Living Theatre, Lion Theatre, Kraine Theater, the Red Room, and at the Kaffileikhusid (Reykjavik). A Fulbright Scholar in Germany, he graduated from Yale College, Columbia Law School, and New School for Drama. His critically acclaimed *In the Summer Pavilion* is being made into a feature film. He is a Contributing Editor at *PAJ: A Journal of Performance and Art* and writes for *Art in America.*